Grade 1

Pearson Scott Foresman
Concept Literacy
Leveled Reader
Teaching Guide

Glenview, Illinois • Boston, Massachusetts • Chandler, Arizona • Upper Saddle River, New Jersey

Accelerated
Reader®

ISBN: 13: 978-0-328-48459-1
ISBN: 10:   0-328-48459-8
5 6 7 8 9 VOYM 16 15 14 13 12
CC1

Table of Contents

CONCEPT LITERACY READER TITLE	Instruction	Blackline Master
In My Room	9	10
I Like My Family	11	12
Outside My Door	13	14
My Friends	15	16
My School	17	18
Around My Neighborhood	19	20
The Dog	21	22
Helping Pets	23	24
Animals Help	25	26
We See Animals	27	28
Neighborhood Animals	29	30
Wild Animals	31	32

Graphic Organizers

Introduction

Pearson Scott Foresman *Reading Street* provides more than 750 leveled readers that help children become better readers and build a lifelong love of reading. The *Reading Street* leveled readers are engaging texts that help children practice critical reading skills and strategies. They also provide opportunities to build vocabulary, understand concepts, and develop fluent reading.

The concept literacy leveled readers were developed to help low-level readers better understand basic concepts and grade-level themes. Most are nonfiction texts using vocabulary that will help develop academic concepts. The concept vocabulary is listed for each lesson. At the early guided reading levels, the text is patterned and repetitive, and there is a very strong picture-text match. The concept literacy leveled readers were developed to be age-appropriate and appealing to children at each grade level.

USING THE LEVELED READERS

You can use the leveled readers to meet the diverse needs of your children. Consider using the readers to

- build fluency
- build vocabulary and concepts
- build background for the main selections in the student book
- provide a variety of reading experiences, e.g., shared, group, individual, take-home, readers' theater

GUIDED READING APPROACH

The *Reading Street* leveled readers are leveled according to Guided Reading criteria by experts trained in Guided Reading. The Guided Reading levels increase in difficulty within a grade level and across grade levels. In addition to leveling according to Guided Reading criteria, the instruction provided in the *Concept Literacy Leveled Reader Teaching Guide* is compatible with Guided Reading instruction. An instructional routine is provided for each leveled reader. This routine is most effective when working with individual children or small groups.

MANAGING THE CLASSROOM

When using the leveled readers with individuals or small groups, you'll want to keep the other children engaged in meaningful, independent learning tasks. Establishing independent practice stations throughout the classroom and child routines for these practice stations can help you manage the rest of the class while you work with individuals or small groups. Practice stations can include listening, phonics, vocabulary, independent reading, and cross-curricular activities. For classroom management, create a work board that lists the practice stations and which children should be at each station. Provide instructions at each station that detail the tasks to be accomplished. Update the board and alert children when they should rotate to a new station. For additional support for managing your classroom, see the *Reading Street* Practice Stations' *Classroom Management Handbook.*

USING THE CONCEPT LITERACY LEVELED READER TEACHING GUIDE

The *Concept Literacy Leveled Reader Teaching Guide* provides an instruction plan for each reader based on the same instructional routine.

INTRODUCE THE BOOK The Introduction includes suggestions for creating interest in the text by discussing the concept, building background, and previewing the book and its features.

READ THE BOOK Before children begin reading the book, have them set purposes for reading. Determine how you want children in a particular group to read the text—softly or silently, to a specific point, or the entire text. Then use the Comprehension Questions to provide support as needed and to assess comprehension.

REVISIT THE BOOK The Think and Share questions provide opportunities for children to demonstrate their understanding of the text and to further develop the target concept. The Response Options require children to revisit the text to respond to what they've read and to move beyond the text to explore related content.

USING THE GRAPHIC ORGANIZERS

Graphic organizers in blackline-master format can be found on pages 81–102. These can be used as overhead transparencies or as worksheets.

EVALUATING PERFORMANCE

Use the evaluation forms that begin on page 7 to make notes about your children's reading skills, use of reading strategies, and general reading behaviors.

READING BEHAVIORS CHECKLIST (p. 7) Provides criteria for monitoring certain reading behaviors.

READING STRATEGY ASSESSMENT (p. 8) Provides criteria for evaluating each child's proficiency as a strategic reader.

Reading Behaviors Checklist

Child's Name _____   Date _____

Behavior	Yes	No	Not Applicable
Recognizes letters of the alphabet			
Recognizes name in print			
Recognizes some environmental print, such as signs and logos			
Knows the difference between letters and words			
Knows the difference between capital and lowercase letters			
Understands function of capitalization and punctuation			
Recognizes that book parts, such as the cover, title page, and table of contents, offer information			
Recognizes that words are represented in writing by specific sequences of letters			
Recognizes words that rhyme			
Distinguishes rhyming and nonrhyming words			
Knows letter-sound correspondences			
Identifies and isolates initial sounds in words			
Identifies and isolates final sounds in words			
Blends sounds to make spoken words			
Segments one-syllable spoken words into individual phonemes			
Reads consonant blends and digraphs			
Reads and understands endings, such as -es, -ed, -ing			
Reads vowels and vowel diphthongs			
Reads and understands possessives			
Reads and understands compound words			
Reads simple sentences			
Reads simple stories			
Understands simple story structure			
Other:			

Reading Strategy Assessment

Child _____ Date _____

Teacher _____

		Proficient	Developing	Emerging	Not showing trait
Building Background Comments:	Previews	☐	☐	☐	☐
	Asks questions	☐	☐	☐	☐
	Predicts	☐	☐	☐	☐
	Activates prior knowledge	☐	☐	☐	☐
	Sets own purposes for reading	☐	☐	☐	☐
	Other:	☐	☐	☐	☐
Comprehension Comments:	Retells/summarizes	☐	☐	☐	☐
	Questions, evaluates ideas	☐	☐	☐	☐
	Relates to self/other texts	☐	☐	☐	☐
	Paraphrases	☐	☐	☐	☐
	Rereads/reads ahead for meaning	☐	☐	☐	☐
	Visualizes	☐	☐	☐	☐
	Uses decoding strategies	☐	☐	☐	☐
	Uses vocabulary strategies	☐	☐	☐	☐
	Understands key ideas of a text	☐	☐	☐	☐
	Other:	☐	☐	☐	☐
Fluency Comments:	Adjusts reading rate	☐	☐	☐	☐
	Reads for accuracy	☐	☐	☐	☐
	Uses expression	☐	☐	☐	☐
	Other:	☐	☐	☐	☐
Connections Comments:	Relates text to self	☐	☐	☐	☐
	Relates text to text	☐	☐	☐	☐
	Relates text to world	☐	☐	☐	☐
	Other:	☐	☐	☐	☐
Self-Assessment Comments:	Is aware of: Strengths	☐	☐	☐	☐
	Needs	☐	☐	☐	☐
	Improvement/achievement	☐	☐	☐	☐
	Sets and implements learning goals	☐	☐	☐	☐
	Maintains logs, records, portfolio	☐	☐	☐	☐
	Works with others	☐	☐	☐	☐
	Shares ideas and materials	☐	☐	☐	☐
	Other:	☐	☐	☐	☐

In My Room

SUMMARY Children read about the special things that are in a child's bedroom.

VOCABULARY
High-Frequency Words
| I | see | a |

Concept Words
| bed | pillow | dresser |
| books | toys | teddy bear |

INTRODUCE THE BOOK

BUILD BACKGROUND Invite children to talk about the special things that are in their rooms.

ELL Pair less-proficient English speakers with proficient English speakers and have them discuss the photos in the book.

PREVIEW Invite children to take a picture walk to preview the text and photos. Ask children to identify the things in the room on each page. Ask why they think these things are important.

READ THE BOOK

SET PURPOSE Have children set a purpose for reading *In My Room*. Ask children to think about their own room and how it is like or different from this room.

COMPREHENSION QUESTIONS

PAGE 3 What do you see on this page? *(a bed)* What kind of a room is this? *(a child's bedroom)*

PAGE 7 Who do you think this room belongs to? Why do you think that? *(Responses will vary.)*

PAGE 8 Do you have a special toy? What is it and why is it special to you? *(Responses will vary.)*

TEXT-TO-SELF QUESTION
What part of this room is your favorite? Why?

REVISIT THE BOOK

THINK AND SHARE
Answers
1. bed, pillow, dresser, books, toys, teddy bear
2. Responses will vary, but might include a special toy, blanket, or teddy bear.
3. Responses will vary depending on the child's toy or activity preference.

EXTEND UNDERSTANDING Discuss the photos in the book. Talk about the many ways that someone might decorate a room for a child. Ask: If you could decorate your room any way you wanted, what would you include?

RESPONSE OPTIONS
WRITING Have children draw a picture of their room. Help children write captions and label the special things in their room.

SOCIAL STUDIES CONNECTION

Provide old magazines and ask children to look for pictures to create a special room. Have children cut out pictures and paste them on construction paper. Help children identify and draw who might like the room that they have created and write labels for their pictures.

GRAPHIC ORGANIZER, PAGE 10
Work with children to complete the web to show the things in their rooms. Children may write words or draw pictures. *(Possible responses: bed, dresser, chair, books, toys, dolls)*

Name_____

Fill in the web to show things in your room.

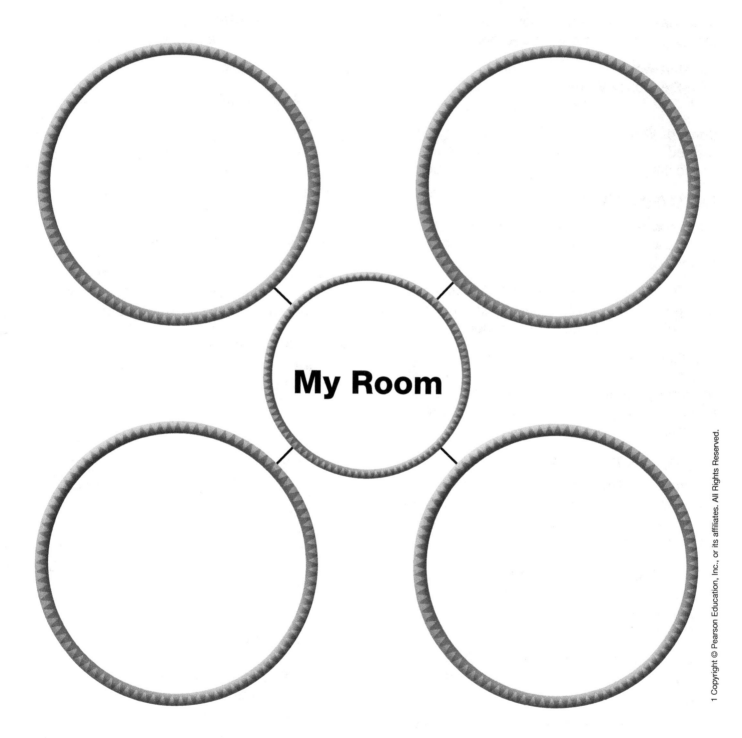

I Like My Family

SUMMARY Children read about a young girl's family and learn about who makes up a family.

VOCABULARY

High-Frequency Words

I	like	my

Concept Words

mom	dad	sister
brother	dog	family

INTRODUCE THE BOOK

BUILD BACKGROUND Invite children to talk about the people in their families.

ELL Have children suggest words for their family members in their home language and in English. Make a list of their suggestions, and help them with any English words that they don't know.

PREVIEW Invite children to take a picture walk to preview the text and photos. Ask children to identify who the person on each page might be.

READ THE BOOK

SET PURPOSE Have children set a purpose for reading *I Like My Family*. Ask children to think about their family and what makes their family the same as or different from the family in the book.

COMPREHENSION QUESTIONS

PAGE 3 Who do you see on this page? *(a girl and her mother)* What is the mother doing? *(Possible response: She is working or paying bills.)*

PAGE 6 Who might this be? *(the girl and her younger brother)* Do you have a little brother or sister? What do you do with him or her? *(Responses will vary.)*

PAGE 8 Count the members of this family. How many people are in your family? *(Responses will vary.)*

TEXT-TO-WORLD QUESTION

What makes this family the same as or different from other families in other places?

REVISIT THE BOOK

THINK AND SHARE

Answers

1. The girl has a mom, dad, sister, brother, and dog in her family.
2. Responses will vary but should include the members of the child's family.
3. Responses will vary depending on the child's family experience.

EXTEND UNDERSTANDING Ask children to think about the many different kinds of families. Who else might be included as a family member? Make a list of the children's ideas.

RESPONSE OPTIONS

WRITING Have children draw a picture of their family. Help them write captions for their illustrations and label each member of their family.

SOCIAL STUDIES CONNECTION

Have children create a poster of their family. Ask them to include their immediate and extended family members as well as pets.

Time For **SOCIAL STUDIES**

GRAPHIC ORGANIZER, PAGE 12

Encourage children to complete the web with drawings that show family members doing special things. Illustrations will vary. *(Possible responses: mom reading a story, dad cooking, sister playing a game, brother helping with a computer, walking the dog together)*

Name_____

Fill in the web to show the people in your family.

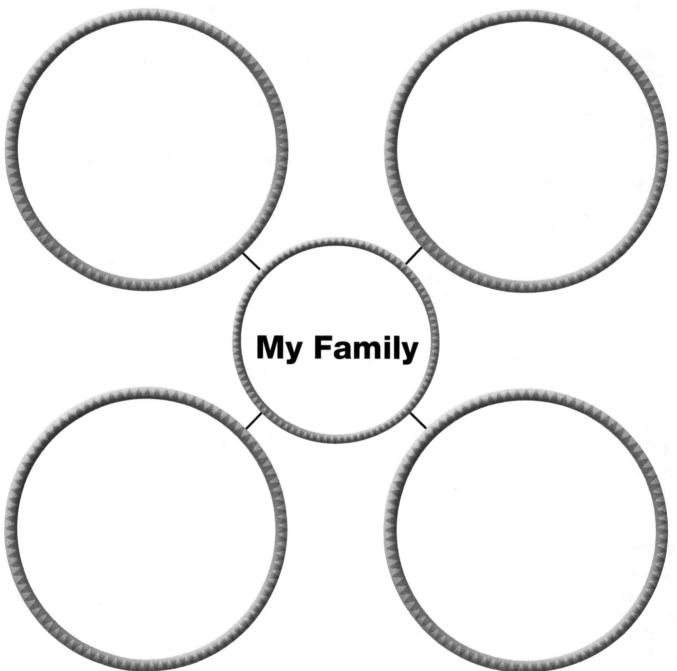

My Family

Outside My Door

SUMMARY Children read and learn about the world right outside their door.

VOCABULARY

High-Frequency Words

do   you
see   the

Concept Words

house   porch   yard
tree   fence   bike

INTRODUCE THE BOOK

BUILD BACKGROUND Invite children to discuss what is outside the door of their homes.

ELL Have children suggest words for such things as *house, porch, yard,* or *garden* in their home language and in English. Make a list of their suggestions, and help them with any English words they don't know.

PREVIEW Invite children to take a picture walk to preview the text and photos. Ask children to identify the things that are outside the door on each page.

READ THE BOOK

SET PURPOSE Have children set a purpose for reading *Outside My Door.* Ask children to think about how their house and yard are like or different from the house and yard in the book.

COMPREHENSION QUESTIONS

PAGE 3 This is a house. Does everyone live in a house? *(No)* Where else might someone live? *(Possible response: an apartment building)*

PAGE 5 What are some things you might find in a yard? *(Possible responses: a swing set, trees, a fence, toys, a garden)* What are some of the things that you can do in a yard? *(Possible responses: play, read, work in the garden)*

PAGE 8 Not everyone has a bike. What other toys might you find in a backyard? *(Possible responses: skates, swing set, balls, tricycle, trucks)*

TEXT-TO-SELF QUESTION

Which things in the book do you have outside your door?

REVISIT THE BOOK

THINK AND SHARE
Answers
1. porch, yard, tree, fence, bike
2. Responses will vary depending on the type of home that a child lives in but should demonstrate knowledge of the word *outside.*
3. Possible response: A porch is often a place to sit with the family.

EXTEND UNDERSTANDING Discuss the photos in the book. Talk about the many different kinds of homes and yards. Then talk about some of the things outside the door at school. Take the class to the front door of the school to observe. Then make a list of what they see.

RESPONSE OPTIONS

WRITING Have children draw a picture of their home. Help children label the things outside their door.

SOCIAL STUDIES CONNECTION

Have children create a mural on butcher paper by illustrating their homes and other things they might see outside their door.

GRAPHIC ORGANIZER, PAGE 14

Work with children to complete the chart showing what's outside their door. They can write or draw the things they see. Help them out by asking, Does your home have a porch? a yard? a fence? and so on.

Name_____

Fill in the chart to show what is outside the door of your home.

What is outside my door?

My Friends

SUMMARY Children read about friends and learn how neighborhood friends play and work together.

VOCABULARY
High-Frequency Words

| I | with | my |

Concept Words

friends	run	jump
hop	climb	ride
rake		

INTRODUCE THE BOOK

BUILD BACKGROUND Invite children to share some of the activities that they enjoy with friends from their neighborhood.

ELL Show pictures of children playing in different neighborhoods such as a city, suburban, and rural community. Ask children to discuss what they see. Have them name the activities in English and in their home language.

PREVIEW Invite children to take a picture walk to preview the text and photos. Ask children to identify the activity and setting on each page.

READ THE BOOK

SET PURPOSE Have children set a purpose for reading. Ask children to think about what they do with their friends and whether those activities are like the ones in the book.

COMPREHENSION QUESTIONS

PAGE 5 What are the children doing on this page? *(The children are playing hopscotch.)* What do you know about hopscotch? How do you play the game? *(Responses will vary.)*

PAGE 6 Where would you be able to play on equipment like the jungle gym on this page? *(Possible response: a park or school playground)*

PAGE 8 Have you ever worked in the yard with your friends? If so, what kind of work did you do? *(Possible responses: rake leaves, plant flowers or vegetables, pull weeds)*

TEXT-TO-SELF QUESTION
Which activities that we read about have you and your friends done together?

REVISIT THE BOOK
THINK AND SHARE
Answers
1. The friends run, jump, hop, climb, ride, and rake.
2. Answers will vary, but should include an activity the child enjoys with his or her friends.
3. Responses will vary depending on the type of weather, community, and resources.

EXTEND UNDERSTANDING Discuss the photos in the book. Talk about the many different ways that children play together in their neighborhoods. Ask: What are some games you play in your neighborhood?

RESPONSE OPTIONS
WRITING Have children choose one of the activities from the book that they might like to participate in with their friends. Have them draw a picture showing themselves doing this activity with their friends. Help children write captions for their illustrations.

SOCIAL STUDIES CONNECTION

Provide old magazines and ask children to look for pictures of children participating together in a variety of activities. Have children cut out pictures and paste them on construction paper. Help them identify the activities that the children are engaged in. Have children write labels for their pictures, and then display them in the classroom.

GRAPHIC ORGANIZER, PAGE 16
Work with children to fill in the web to show some of the activities they enjoy sharing with friends in their neighborhood. *(Possible responses: biking, playing ball, playing tag, jumping rope)*

Name_____

Fill in the web to show what you and your friends do together in your neighborhood.

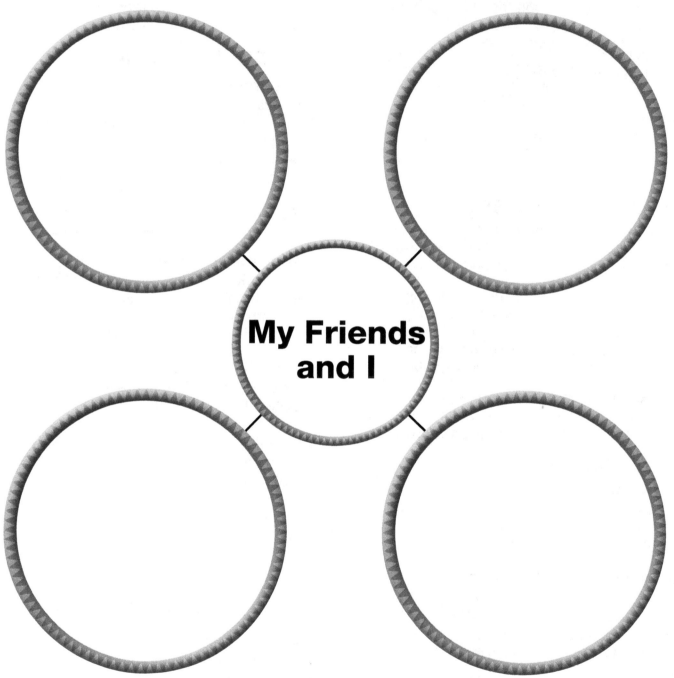

My Friends and I

My School

SUMMARY Children read about the things in their school world.

VOCABULARY
High-Frequency Words
this   is   my

Concept Words
school bus   school   playground
desk   teacher   class

INTRODUCE THE BOOK

BUILD BACKGROUND Invite children to talk about their school and the things around them at school.

ELL Have children suggest words for *school, teacher, playground, desk,* and *class* in their home language and in English. Make a list of their suggestions, and help them with any English words that they don't know.

PREVIEW Invite children to take a picture walk to preview the text and photos. Ask children to identify the things in the book that they also have at their school.

READ THE BOOK

SET PURPOSE Have children set a purpose for reading *My School.* Ask children to think about how their school is like or different from the school in the book.

COMPREHENSION QUESTIONS

PAGE 3 What do you see on this page? *(a school bus)* What is another way that some children might get to school? *(Possible responses: walk, car, bike)*

PAGE 5 What are some things you might see on a playground? *(Possible responses: trees, fence, jungle gym, swings, children)* What can you do on a playground? *(Possible responses: play, read, talk, run, climb, slide)*

PAGE 6 Do you have a desk like this one? What are some things in your desk? *(Possible responses: books, paper, pencils, crayons)*

TEXT-TO-WORLD QUESTION

How might schools in other places be different from this one?

REVISIT THE BOOK

THINK AND SHARE
Answers
1. Responses will vary but should make note of the similarities.
2. Responses will vary but might include cafeteria, gym, music room, playground, library, principal's office.
3. Responses will vary depending on the child's preference for school activities.

EXTEND UNDERSTANDING Discuss the photos in the book and the different areas in a school. Take the class on a walk around the school and talk about why each part of the school is important.

RESPONSE OPTIONS

WRITING Have children draw a picture of their classroom. Help children label their illustrations.

SOCIAL STUDIES CONNECTION
Have children create a mural on butcher paper with each child illustrating a different part of the school.

Time For SOCIAL STUDIES

GRAPHIC ORGANIZER, PAGE 18
Work with children to complete the web to show the things in their school. Children may write words or draw pictures. *(Possible responses: school bus, desk, office, library, gym, teacher, classmates)*

Name_____

Fill in the web to show things at your school.

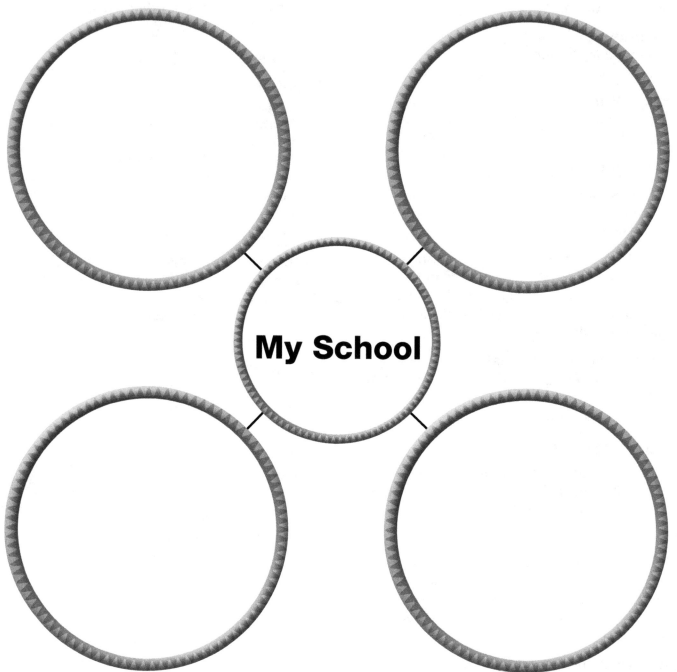

My School

18

Around My Neighborhood

SUMMARY Children read and learn about the businesses in a neighborhood.

VOCABULARY
High-Frequency Words
we   go   to
the

Concept Words
grocery store   post office
library   bank
laundromat   farmers market

INTRODUCE THE BOOK

BUILD BACKGROUND Invite children to talk about the shops and businesses that they go to in their neighborhood.

ELL Pair less-proficient English speakers with proficient English speakers and have them discuss the photos in the book.

PREVIEW Invite children to take a picture walk to preview the text and photos. Ask children whether they go to places like these in their neighborhood.

READ THE BOOK

SET PURPOSE Have children set a purpose for reading *Around My Neighborhood*. Ask children to think about how this neighborhood is like their own neighborhood.

COMPREHENSION QUESTIONS

PAGE 3 What do you see on this page? *(a grocery store)* What kinds of things will you find at a grocery store? *(Possible responses: cereal, meat, milk, dog food)*

PAGE 5 Where is the family in this photo? *(They are at the library.)* What do you do at the library? *(Possible response: get books, get videos, use the computer)*

PAGE 8 This is a farmers market. What might a farmer sell at a farmers market? *(Possible response: tomatoes, peaches, apples, corn)*

TEXT-TO-WORLD QUESTION
Which places in the book would you like to visit in your neighborhood?

REVISIT THE BOOK
THINK AND SHARE
Answers
1. grocery store, post office, library, bank, laundromat, farmers market
2. Responses will vary but might include a toy store, restaurant, or department store.
3. Responses will vary depending on the child's family activities and neighborhood businesses.

EXTEND UNDERSTANDING Discuss the photos in the book. Talk about the many different businesses in a community. Discuss the importance of having the people who live in a neighborhood come to and use these businesses.

RESPONSE OPTIONS
DRAMA Have children role-play a visit to one or more businesses in their neighborhood. Children can take the parts of a parent and child as they make their visits. Have children explain what takes place during each visit.

SOCIAL STUDIES CONNECTION
On a large chart, create a map of the neighborhood or an area around the school. Have children suggest some nearby businesses to locate on the map. Label each business, and then post the map in your classroom.

GRAPHIC ORGANIZER, PAGE 20
Work with children to complete the web showing a variety of places in their neighborhood. Children may write words or draw pictures. *(Possible responses: grocery store, post office, pet store, library, bank, laundromat, farmers market, restaurant)*

Name_____

Fill in the web to show places in your neighborhood.

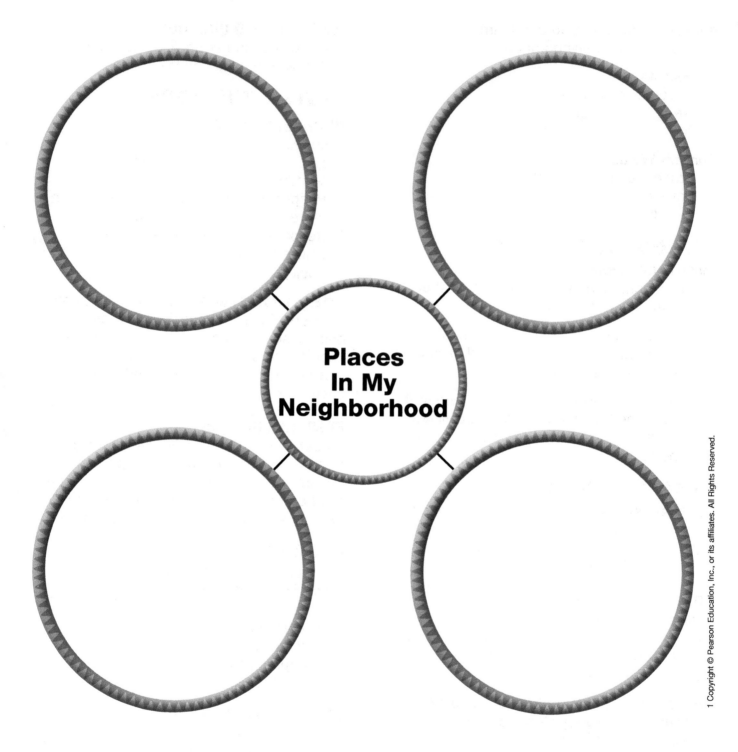

Places In My Neighborhood

The Dog

SUMMARY Children read about a dog and learn that animals need certain things to survive.

VOCABULARY
High-Frequency Words
a   the

Concept Words
dog	food	water
home	bed	toys
friend		

INTRODUCE THE BOOK

BUILD BACKGROUND Invite children to share what they know about dogs. If any children have dogs at home, ask them to discuss what their pets need.

ELL Have children suggest words for pets in their home-language and in English. Make a list of their suggestions, and help them with any English words they don't know.

PREVIEW Invite children to take a picture walk to preview the text and illustrations. Have them discuss what is pictured with the dog on each page. Ask children why they think the dog might need each of these things.

READ THE BOOK

SET PURPOSE Have children set a purpose for reading *The Dog*. Ask them to think about the things a dog needs and who might provide these things for the dog.

COMPREHENSION QUESTIONS

PAGE 3 What is the dog doing on this page? *(The dog is eating.)*

PAGE 4 What part of the body does a dog use to drink water? *(tongue, mouth)*

PAGE 7 What does the dog have on this page? *(toys)* Why might a dog need toys? *(Possible response: A dog needs to run and play every day to be healthy.)*

TEXT-TO-SELF QUESTION
How is what a dog needs every day like what you need every day?

REVISIT THE BOOK
THINK AND SHARE
Answers
1. food, water, a home, a bed, toys, a friend; Possible response: The dog needs these things to live and be healthy.
2. Possible response: The dog got these things from its owner.
3. Responses will vary depending on the type of pet but should demonstrate knowledge of the word *responsible* and reflect the notion of kindness and the needs of pets.

EXTEND UNDERSTANDING Ask children to think of other things a pet might need. Make a list of the children's ideas.

RESPONSE OPTIONS
WRITING Have children create more pages that might belong in this book. Have them draw a picture, and help them write a sentence to go with it, such as *The dog has a leash.*

SCIENCE CONNECTION
Display nonfiction books about taking care of pets. Suggest that children look through the books to find  facts about pet care. Encourage children to share their facts with classmates, illustrate them, and compile a class booklet about pets.

GRAPHIC ORGANIZER, PAGE 22
Work with children to fill in the web to show what pets need. Children may write words or draw pictures. *(Possible responses: food, water, shelter, exercise, brushing, washing, petting, love)*

Name_____

Fill in the web to tell what pets need.

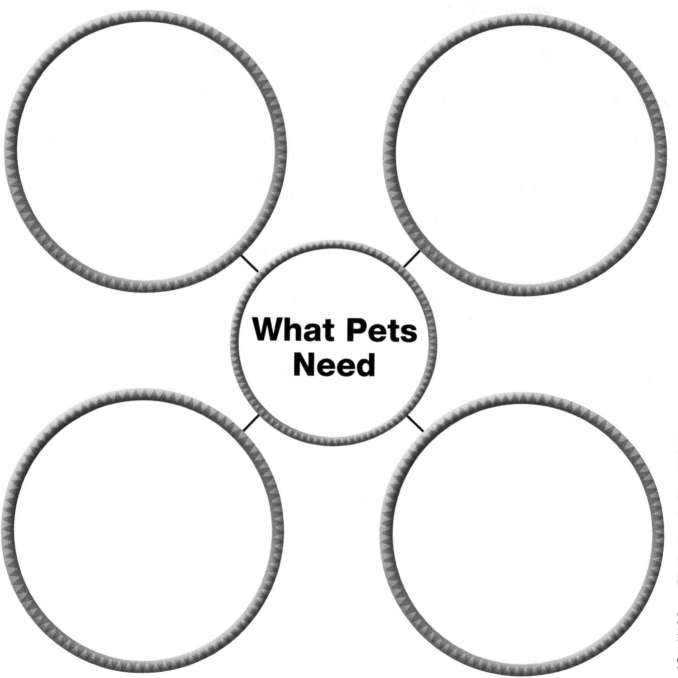

What Pets Need

Helping Pets

SUMMARY Children read about pets and learn about ways that people can help them.

VOCABULARY

High-Frequency Words

a   the

Concept Words

helps   pet   vet

INTRODUCE THE BOOK

BUILD BACKGROUND Invite children to share what they know about pets. If any of the children have pets at home, ask them to discuss how they help their pets.

ELL Have children suggest home-language and English words for pet care, such as *brush, wash, feed,* and so on. Write the English words on note cards and help students pronounce them. Students can use the note cards for practice.

PREVIEW Invite children to take a picture walk to preview the text and illustrations. Have children discuss how each person is helping a pet. Ask children why they think these pets need help.

READ THE BOOK

SET PURPOSE Have children set a purpose for reading *Helping Pets*. Ask children to think about how people might help their pets.

COMPREHENSION QUESTIONS

PAGE 4 How is the girl helping the pet on this page? *(The girl is feeding the pet bird.)*

PAGE 6 What part of the pet is the vet looking at on this page? *(teeth)* Why is this important? *(Pets, like people, need their teeth checked to be healthy.)*

PAGE 8 Why do you think the man is helping this pet? *(Possible response: The horse needs its hooves checked and its shoes changed to stay healthy.)*

TEXT-TO-WORLD QUESTION

In what ways do both pets and people need help?

REVISIT THE BOOK

THINK AND SHARE
Answers
1. Responses will vary, but children should support their answers with reasons.
2. Answers will vary, but children might suggest giving them exercise, feeding them, training them, taking care of injured animals, and so on.
3. Responses will vary but should demonstrate knowledge of the word *careers,* and children should support their answers with reasons.

EXTEND UNDERSTANDING Ask children to explain why they think it is important to help pets and take care of them. Make a list of the children's suggestions.

RESPONSE OPTIONS

DRAMA Have children act out other ways they can help pets. Classmates can guess what each "actor" is doing.

SOCIAL STUDIES CONNECTION

Display some nonfiction books about careers in pet care. Suggest that children look through the books and choose a career they are particularly interested in. Have them draw a picture that illustrates the career and how it helps pets or animals.

GRAPHIC ORGANIZER, PAGE 24

Have children complete the chart to tell what they read. They can draw a simple picture or write a word to fill in the last column. *(Responses: cat–brush, bird–feed, dog–wash, dog–check-up, dog–haircut, horse–fix shoes)*

Name_____

Fill in the chart to tell how each person helps.

Pet	Who helps?	How?
cat	boy	
bird	girl	
dog	family	
dog	vet	
dog	woman	
horse	man	

Animals Help

SUMMARY Children read about animals and the ways animals help people.

VOCABULARY
High-Frequency Words
a   help

Concept Words
dog   hen   camel
horse   cow   monkey

INTRODUCE THE BOOK

BUILD BACKGROUND Invite children to share what they know about the ways in which animals help people.

ELL Have children give their home-language names for the animals in the book. Write the words on note cards. Write the English names for the animals on another set of note cards. Have children play a matching game with the cards.

PREVIEW Invite children to take a picture walk to preview the text and illustrations. Have children discuss how each animal is helping. Ask children why they think people sometimes need animals to help them.

READ THE BOOK

SET PURPOSE Have children set a purpose for reading *Animals Help*. Ask children to think about ways in which they might need help from an animal.

COMPREHENSION QUESTIONS

PAGE 4 How is the horse helping the people on this page? (*The horse is pulling a plow in a farm field.*)

PAGE 6 How is the cow helping on this page? (*The cow is giving milk that we drink.*)

PAGE 8 Why do you think the person on this page needs the monkey's help? (*Possible response: This person is not be able to do some things for herself.*)

TEXT-TO-WORLD QUESTION
What animals do you know of that help people by producing food to eat?

REVISIT THE BOOK
THINK AND SHARE
Answers
1. Possible responses: A dog can be a guide for blind people, fetch slippers or other objects, keep you company, warn you of intruders, or be a friend.
2. A hen produces eggs we eat, and a cow produces milk we drink.
3. Possible responses: horse, camel, mule, ox, donkey, elephants

EXTEND UNDERSTANDING Ask children to explain ways in which they have been helped by an animal. Make a list of the children's ideas.

RESPONSE OPTIONS
WRITING Have children each choose an animal from the book and write a card thanking the animal for its help. Suggest that children illustrate their cards.

SOCIAL STUDIES CONNECTION

Have children work together to create a poster of how animals help people. Have them draw pictures of animals helping people or cut out pictures from old magazines. Help them paste each picture on the poster and label it.

GRAPHIC ORGANIZER, PAGE 26
Work with children to fill in the web to show how animals help people. Children may write words or draw pictures. (*Possible responses: guiding a person who is blind, providing food, pulling heavy equipment, getting a newspaper, providing transportation, being a friend, protecting people*)

Name_____

Fill in the web to tell how animals help people.

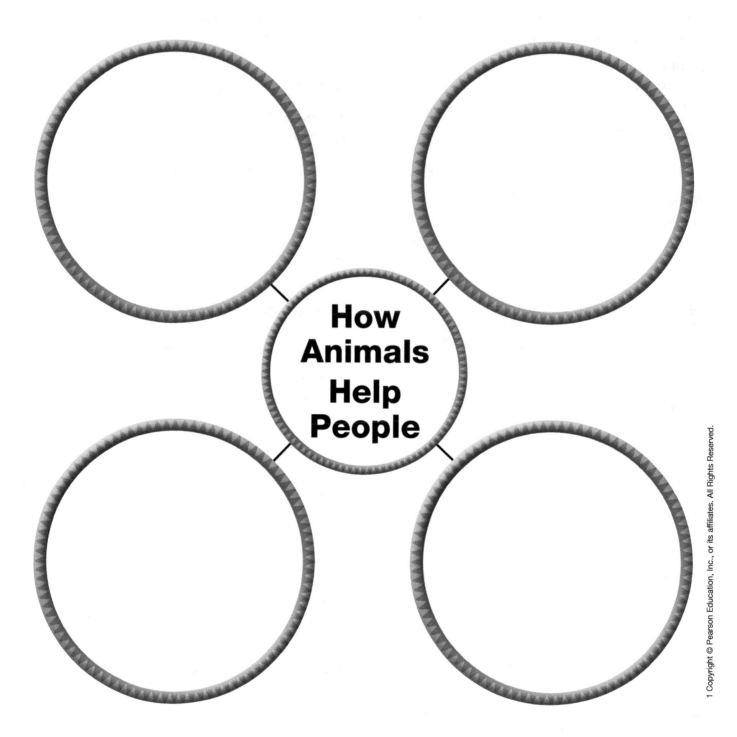

How Animals Help People

We See Animals

SUMMARY Children read and learn about how observing animals helps us know more about them.

VOCABULARY

High-Frequency Words

| eat | see | this | we |

Concept Words

| animals | run | play |
| drink | sleep | |

INTRODUCE THE BOOK

BUILD BACKGROUND Invite children to share what they know about things animals do—how they move, where they live and sleep, how they run and play, and so on.

ELL Pair less-proficient English speakers with proficient English speakers and have them discuss the photos in the book.

PREVIEW Invite children to take a picture walk to preview the text and illustrations. Have children what the animals are doing on each page. Ask why they think it's important to watch animals.

READ THE BOOK

SET PURPOSE Have children set a purpose for reading. Ask children to think about what they would like to learn from watching animals.

COMPREHENSION QUESTIONS

PAGE 3 What animals do you see on this page? *(a deer and a squirrel)* What other animals might be nearby? *(Possible responses: a bird, a rabbit, a fox)*

PAGE 7 Where would you go to see this animal sleeping? *(Possible responses: a field or prairie)* Where else could you observe animals sleeping? *(at a zoo, in a forest)*

PAGE 8 Look at the cat playing on this page. What else might you see this animal do? *(Possible responses: eat, sleep, run)*

TEXT-TO-SELF QUESTION

How is what animals do every day like what you do every day?

REVISIT THE BOOK

THINK AND SHARE
Answers
1. Possible responses: We can learn about what and how animals eat, what games they like to play, how they move, and how they take care of their babies.
2. Possible response: We might find out what animals like to play with, how they get along with other animals, how they make friends.
3. Responses will vary but should demonstrate knowledge of the word *observe*.

EXTEND UNDERSTANDING Discuss the book's illustrations. Talk about how someone might go about observing animals. Ask: If you were going to observe animals, where would you go? What tools would you need?

RESPONSE OPTIONS

ART Have children choose one of the animals from the book and draw a picture of it doing something else. Help children write captions for their illustrations.

SCIENCE CONNECTION

Provide old magazines and ask children to look through them for pictures of animals doing things. Have children cut out the pictures and paste them on construction paper. Help children write labels for their pictures.

GRAPHIC ORGANIZER, PAGE 28

Work with children to fill in the web to show various activities that we might observe animals doing. *(Possible responses: eat, drink, sleep, run, walk, play, sit, lie down, take care of their babies)*

Name_____

Fill in the web to tell what you can watch animals do.

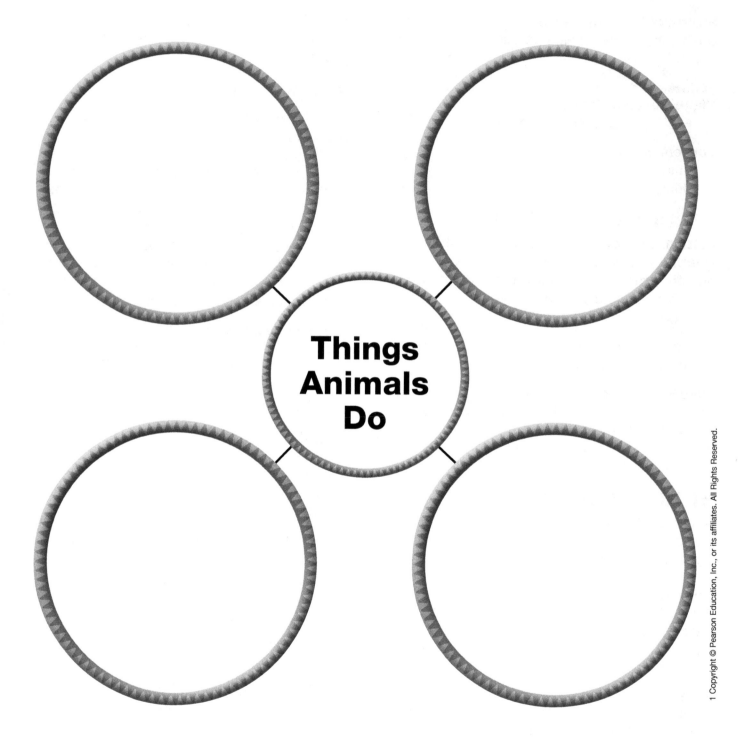

Things
Animals
Do

Neighborhood Animals

SUMMARY Children read about wild animals they might see in their neighborhood.

VOCABULARY
High-Frequency Words
a   here   is

Concept Words
bird   butterfly   rabbit
squirrel   bee   snake

INTRODUCE THE BOOK

BUILD BACKGROUND Invite children to share what they know about animals in their neighborhood. Ask children to tell about the animals they may have seen near their homes.

ELL Show pictures of familiar neighborhood animals. Help children name the animals. Write each word on the board.

PREVIEW Invite children to take a picture walk to preview the text and illustrations. Have children discuss the animals they see. Ask children where they think these animals live.

READ THE BOOK

SET PURPOSE Have children set a purpose for reading *Neighborhood Animals*. Ask them what they think they will find out.

COMPREHENSION QUESTIONS

PAGE 4 What is the squirrel doing on this page? *(The squirrel is eating.)* How does a squirrel find food in the neighborhood? *(Possible response: It might look near trees and shrubs for nuts and berries.)*

PAGE 5 Look at the butterfly on this page. What other animals might you see near flowers in your yard? *(Possible responses: bees, rabbits, birds, worms)*

PAGE 8 How are the animals in this book the same? *(Possible response: They are all small animals—small enough to live easily in the neighborhood.)*

TEXT-TO-SELF QUESTION
Which animals in this book have you seen in your own neighborhood?

REVISIT THE BOOK

THINK AND SHARE
Answers
1. Possible response: Animals live and make their homes in our yards and around our houses. They are part of the neighborhood just like we are.
2. Possible response: They find their food outside—nuts, leaves, berries, insects—and they sleep in nests that they build.
3. Responses will vary.

EXTEND UNDERSTANDING After children have read the book, lead a discussion about the illustrations. Discuss the many animals that live together in one neighborhood. Have children think about how animals in a neighborhood are like people in a neighborhood.

RESPONSE OPTIONS
WRITING Have children write a sentence or two about the animals they have seen in their neighborhoods. They might tell what animals they saw, where the animals were, or what the animals were doing.

SCIENCE CONNECTION
Have children create a mural showing the neighborhood around the school. Have them include on the mural pictures of animals they have seen around the school.

GRAPHIC ORGANIZER, PAGE 30
Work with children to write or draw on the chart the animals they might see in their neighborhood in a tree, in a garden, or in a bush. *(Possible responses: In a tree—bird, squirrel, bugs; In a garden—bird, bee, rabbit, snake, butterfly, gopher, ant, worm; In a bush—bird, squirrel, butterfly, bugs)*

Name_____

List the animals you might find in these spots in your neighborhood.
Write words or draw pictures.

Animals in My Neighborhood

Wild Animals

SUMMARY Children read about animals that live all around the world.

VOCABULARY
High-Frequency Words

a	here	is

Concept Words

tiger	parrot	polar bear
giraffe	dolphin	lizard

INTRODUCE THE BOOK

BUILD BACKGROUND Invite children to share what they know about wild animals. If any of the children have seen wild animals, ask them to talk about their experiences.

ELL Pair less-proficient English speakers with proficient English speakers and have them discuss the photos in the book. Encourage children to use the names of the animals and discuss them.

PREVIEW Invite children to take a picture walk to preview the text and illustrations. Have children discuss the names of the wild animals on each page. Ask children where they think each of these animals lives.

READ THE BOOK

SET PURPOSE Have children set a purpose for reading *Wild Animals*. Ask children to think about wild animals that they have seen in zoos, in books, or on TV.

COMPREHENSION QUESTIONS

PAGE 5 Where might you go to see a parrot? *(Possible response: to a jungle)* What might we do to keep wild parrots or other rare birds safe? *(Possible response: not capture or hunt them)*

PAGE 6 What kind of environment do you think a dolphin lives in? How can you tell from this picture? *(in water; The dolphin is jumping out of the water in this picture.)*

TEXT-TO-TEXT QUESTION

How are these animals like neighborhood animals you have read about? How are they different?

REVISIT THE BOOK

THINK AND SHARE
Answers
1. No. Possible responses: It is too big. It would not be able to find a place to sleep. It wouldn't find enough food. It probably couldn't survive around so many people.
2. No. Possible responses: A lizard needs warm temperatures. It is cold where polar bears live. A lizard would not survive.
3. Responses will vary.

EXTEND UNDERSTANDING Lead a discussion about wild animals. Ask volunteers to point out their favorite wild animal from the book. Ask: Why is this animal your favorite?

RESPONSE OPTIONS

SPEAKING AND LISTENING Have children suppose they are guides at the zoo. Ask them to talk about each animal from the story as if they were telling someone about it.

SOCIAL STUDIES CONNECTION

Display nonfiction books about wild animals. Have children look through the books and then work in small groups to create their own "Wild Animal" books. Have them draw pictures of animals in their habitats and write labels or captions to go with them.

GRAPHIC ORGANIZER, PAGE 32
Work with children to complete the web to show a variety of wild animals or their habitats. Children may write words or draw pictures. *(Possible responses: tiger, giraffe, parrot, dolphin, polar bear, lizard, jungle, ocean, desert)*

Name_____

Fill in the web to tell about wild animals.

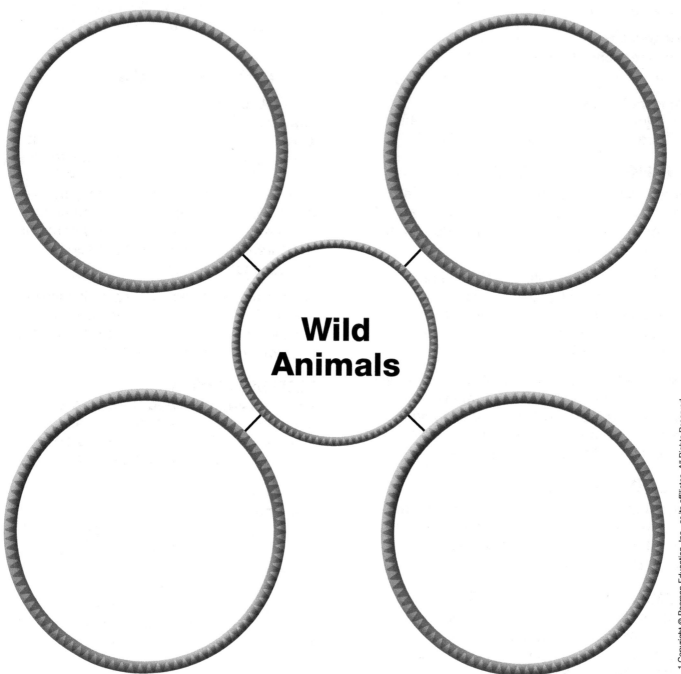

Wild Animals

My Family

SUMMARY Children read about a variety of activities that families enjoy doing together.

VOCABULARY
High-Frequency Words
eats   my

Concept Words
family   shops   plays
together   works   reads

INTRODUCE THE BOOK

BUILD BACKGROUND Discuss with children the various people who might make up a family. Ask children to share the kinds of things they enjoy doing with their families.

ELL Ask children to share home-language and English words for family members, such as *mother, father, sister, brother.* Write home-language and English words on the board.

PREVIEW Invite children to take a picture walk to preview the text and illustrations. Have children discuss what the families are doing together on each page.

READ THE BOOK

SET PURPOSE Have children set a purpose for reading. Ask them to think about how different families might spend time together.

COMPREHENSION QUESTIONS

PAGE 3 What meal do you think this family is eating together? *(lunch or dinner)* Why is it good to eat together as a family? *(Meals are a good time to talk together—to discuss the day's events or to make plans for the next day.)*

PAGE 6 What kind of work is this family doing together? *(gardening)* Do you think they like what they're doing? How can you tell? *(Yes. They are all smiling.)*

PAGE 7 This family is playing football together. What kinds of games do you like to play with your family? *(Responses will vary.)*

TEXT-TO-SELF QUESTION
Which activity from the book would you choose as your favorite? Why?

REVISIT THE BOOK
THINK AND SHARE
Answers
1. Responses will vary, but children should recognize that all could be done alone. However, some activities would be more fun or be accomplished faster when done together.
2. Responses will vary.
3. Possible responses: shopping, working; These are things that must get done if we are to have food to eat and a nice house to live in. The others are more fun, and we can choose to do them or not.

EXTEND UNDERSTANDING Ask children to explain why they think it is important for families to spend time together. Make a list of the children's suggestions.

RESPONSE OPTIONS
DRAMA Have children act out other activities they enjoy doing with their families. Classmates can guess what each "actor" is doing.

SOCIAL STUDIES CONNECTION
Ask children to talk to a friend or neighbor to find out what kinds of activities that person enjoys doing with his or her family. Have children make a list of their findings.

Time For SOCIAL STUDIES

GRAPHIC ORGANIZER, PAGE 34
Have children complete the Main Idea chart to show what families do together. They can draw a simple picture or write a word to fill in each box with a detail. *(Possible responses: eat, walk, shop, work, play, read)*

Name_____

Fill in the chart to show what families do.

Families do many things together.

At School

SUMMARY Children read about activities they do together at school. They will talk about what they learn from working in groups.

VOCABULARY
High-Frequency Words

at	we

Concept Words

read	sing	write
together	paint	play
school		

INTRODUCE THE BOOK

BUILD BACKGROUND Invite children to talk about activities they do as a group at school. Ask children to share what they learn from doing these activities.

PREVIEW Invite children to take a picture walk to preview the text and illustrations. Have the class discuss what the children are doing together on each page. Ask children if they also do these things at school.

READ THE BOOK

Have children set a purpose for reading. Ask them to think about how they spend their time at school each day.

COMPREHENSION QUESTIONS

PAGE 3 Why is it sometimes helpful to read together? *(Friends can help you learn words you don't know.)*

PAGE 4 What can children learn from talking together? *(Possible response: Children can learn to share ideas and to listen to others.)*

PAGE 6 Why do you think these children are painting together? *(Possible responses: because it's more fun to work together; because they want to finish more quickly)*

TEXT-TO-WORLD QUESTION

How is working together at school like working together at home?

REVISIT THE BOOK

THINK AND SHARE
Answers

1. Possible responses: They will learn to get along with one another. They will learn to take turns.
2. Possible responses: They should listen politely when others speak; they should take turns; they should respect the work of others.
3. Possible response: Both a school and a neighborhood need people doing their jobs to run smoothly.

ELL Have children work together in groups to dramatize an activity from the book. Ask children to name each activity.

EXTEND UNDERSTANDING Have children discuss other group activities they do at school, such as eating lunch or going to an all-school assembly. Ask children what they can learn from these activities.

RESPONSE OPTIONS

WRITING Have children create one more page that might belong in this book, such as *We eat together at school.* Ask children to illustrate the page.

SOCIAL STUDIES CONNECTION

Help children make a list that tells why students should work together. Then explain that sometimes it is a good idea to work alone. Work with children to create a list that tells why or when students should work alone.

GRAPHIC ORGANIZER, PAGE 36

Work with children to complete the web to show activities they do together at school. They can draw a simple picture or write a word. *(Possible responses: eat, walk, paint, work, play, read, talk, sing, write)*

Name_____

Fill in the web to show what you do at school.

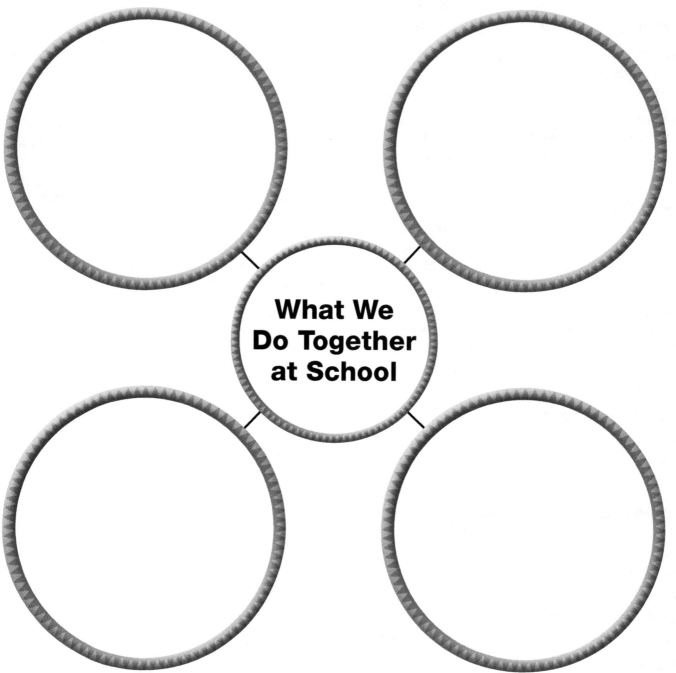

What We Do Together at School

In My Neighborhood

SUMMARY Children read and learn about the people who work in their neighborhood and how these people make the neighborhood a nice place in which to live.

VOCABULARY
High-Frequency Words

a   is   this

Concept Words

police officer   bus driver
firefighter   librarian
mail carrier   teacher

INTRODUCE THE BOOK

BUILD BACKGROUND Invite children to talk about the people who work in their neighborhood. Ask children what these people do to make their neighborhood a nice place.

PREVIEW Invite children to take a picture walk to preview the text and illustrations. Have children discuss the person on each page and what that person does for his or her job.

READ THE BOOK

SET PURPOSE Have children set a purpose for reading *In My Neighborhood*. Ask children to think about their neighborhood and what makes it a nice place to live in.

COMPREHENSION QUESTIONS

PAGE 3 How does a police officer help people in the neighborhood? (*Possible response: A police officer helps keep people safe.*)

PAGE 4 What is important about a firefighter's job? (*Possible response: Firefighters help save people and buildings from fire.*)

PAGE 7 What kinds of things does a librarian do? (*A librarian helps people find information and helps people check out books.*)

TEXT-TO-WORLD QUESTION

Why is it important for our neighborhood to be a nice place?

REVISIT THE BOOK
THINK AND SHARE
Answers
1. Possible responses: They all help the community run smoothly. They help us in many different ways. Some protect us. Some give us information. And others take us places.
2. Responses will vary but should include some community workers.
3. Possible response: We wouldn't get important mail, such as letters from family and friends far away, checks, and so on.

ELL Have children look through magazines for pictures of people they might see in their neighborhood. Ask them to name the people. If necessary, supply the names in English.

EXTEND UNDERSTANDING Have children discuss other people who live and work in their neighborhood. Ask them to tell what these people do to make their neighborhood special.

RESPONSE OPTIONS

ART Help children create a poster-sized map of the area surrounding the school. Have them include people who work in the neighborhood. They can draw or paste magazine pictures of neighborhood workers on the map.

SOCIAL STUDIES CONNECTION
Have children discuss the many types of jobs people have in their neighborhoods. Ask them to think of a job they might like to do and draw a picture of themselves doing it.

Time For SOCIAL STUDIES

GRAPHIC ORGANIZER, PAGE 38
Work with children to complete the chart to show who works in their neighborhood. Children can draw a simple picture or write a word to fill in the chart. (*Responses: librarian; police officer; mail carrier; teacher; firefighter; bus driver*)

Name_____

Fill in the chart to show who works in your neighborhood.

People in My Neighborhood	What They Need

Animals Work Together

SUMMARY Children read about how animals work together to survive.

VOCABULARY
High-Frequency Words
the   work

Concept Words
together   birds   beavers
ants   squirrels   elephants
bees

INTRODUCE THE BOOK

BUILD BACKGROUND Invite children to talk about how animals must work together to survive. Ask them to give examples of animals they can think of that work together in groups.

ELL Write some animal names on note cards, including those in the book. On another set of cards, paste pictures of the animals. Have children match each word card with its picture card.

PREVIEW Invite children to take a picture walk to preview the text and illustrations. Have children discuss the animals on each page and how they are working together.

READ THE BOOK

SET PURPOSE Have children set a purpose for reading *Animals Work Together*. Ask children to think about why animals must work together to survive.

COMPREHENSION QUESTIONS

PAGE 4 What do you think the bees are working together to do? *(make honey)*

PAGE 5 How is the grown-up bird helping the baby survive? *(The grown-up bird is feeding the baby bird.)* Why is this important? *(The baby cannot feed itself.)*

PAGE 6 These squirrels are working together to gather food. What else might squirrels work together to do? *(Possible responses: protect each other, build a nest)*

TEXT-TO-SELF QUESTION

How is the work that animals do together like the work you do with classmates at school?

REVISIT THE BOOK

THINK AND SHARE
Answers
1. Possible response: Each animal has a job to do. This makes their community run smoothly, just like a neighborhood of people.
2. Possible responses: They protect one another. They find food for everyone. They build homes for everyone.
3. Responses will vary but should demonstrate knowledge of the word *protect*.

EXTEND UNDERSTANDING Have children discuss other animals that work together. Ask children to tell how these animals help each other survive.

RESPONSE OPTIONS

WRITING Have children write and illustrate a sentence or two about the importance of animals working together to help one another.

SCIENCE CONNECTION

Have children discuss the characteristics of the animals in the book. Have children list each animal, its charac-  teristics, and how these characteristics help the animal do its job. For example, an ant is an insect with six legs, which help it move quickly.

GRAPHIC ORGANIZER, PAGE 40

Have children complete the chart to tell what these animals do to work together. Children can draw a simple picture or write a sentence to complete the chart. *(Responses: Ants carry leaves. Bees make honey. Birds feed their babies. Squirrels gather food. Beavers build a home. Elephants protect their young.)*

Name_____

Fill in the chart to tell how these animals work together.

Animals	What They Do

In the Forest

SUMMARY Children read about plants and animals that live together in the forest.

VOCABULARY

High-Frequency Words

the   live   tree

Concept Words

forest   birds   bears
plants   deer

INTRODUCE THE BOOK

BUILD BACKGROUND Invite children to talk about the plants and animals they know that live together in the forest. Ask children to discuss other places where they have seen plants and animals living together.

ELL Have children look at the book again. Ask them to make a new book by creating their own illustrations and writing the plant and animal words on each page, in English and in their home languages.

PREVIEW Invite children to take a picture walk to preview the text and illustrations. Have them discuss the plants and animals on each page and tell which they have seen.

READ THE BOOK

SET PURPOSE Have children set a purpose for reading *In the Forest*. Ask them to think about how plants and animals form a community.

COMPREHENSION QUESTIONS

PAGE 3 Why are big trees important in a forest? *(Big trees provide food, shade, and shelter for animals and other plants.)*

PAGE 5 Here are birds in a rain forest. What other birds might live in a forest? *(Possible responses: eagles, hawks, woodpeckers, owls)*

PAGE 7 This picture shows deer living among the plants. How might these plants help the deer? *(Possible responses: The plants provide shelter, protection, and food for the deer.)*

TEXT-TO-WORLD QUESTION

In what other kinds of places have you seen plants and animals living together?

REVISIT THE BOOK

THINK AND SHARE
Answers
1. Possible responses: Deer need trees so that they can eat the leaves and bark. They might also hide behind low, leafy branches. Birds need bugs and berries to eat.
2. Possible responses: birds, bugs, squirrels, trees, flowers
3. Possible responses: It would be harder for them to find food. Birds would not have a place to build their nests.

EXTEND UNDERSTANDING Have children discuss other plants and animals that live in the forest. Ask children to tell how these plants and animals help each other.

RESPONSE OPTIONS

ART Have children draw or paint a picture of a forest that includes plants and animals such as those featured in the book. Encourage children to add other plants and animals.

SCIENCE CONNECTION

Have children think about how a forest community is different from a desert community. How are they the same? Have children look in books to find out which plants would live together in the desert.

GRAPHIC ORGANIZER, PAGE 42

Have children complete the web with plants and animals that live together in the forest. Children can draw simple pictures or write words to fill in the web. *(Possible responses: big trees, little plants, owls, birds, bugs, deer, bears, raccoons, squirrels, chipmunks)*

Name_____

Fill in the web to show plants and animals that live in the forest.

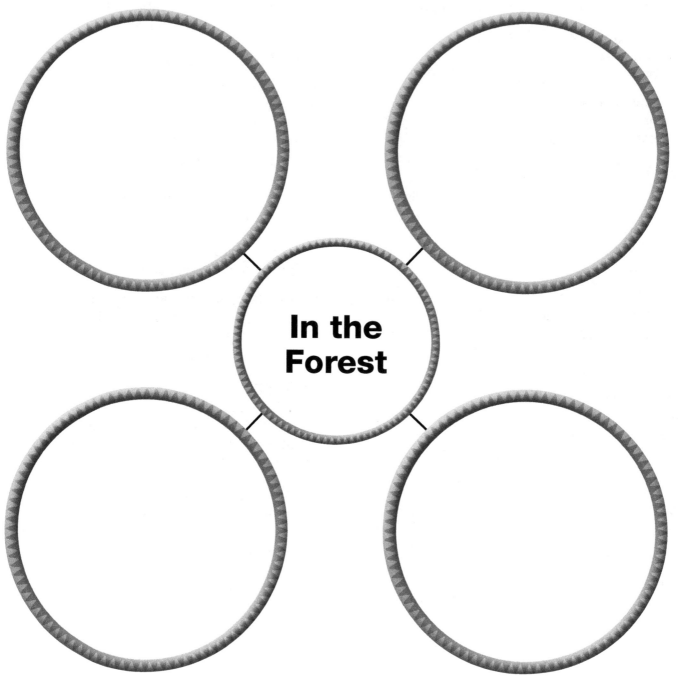

In the Forest

Ants and People

SUMMARY Children read about the similarities between a community of ants and a community of people.

VOCABULARY
High-Frequency Words

eat	we
home	work

Concept Words

build	ants	together

INTRODUCE THE BOOK

BUILD BACKGROUND Invite children to discuss the activities ants do in their communities. Then talk about the activities people do in their communities. How are they the same?

ELL Write verbs from the story on the board—*build, eat, work*. Add others to the list *(walk, run, sleep)*. Have children act out the words to check their comprehension.

PREVIEW Invite children to take a picture walk to preview the text and illustrations. Talk about what is happening on each page.

READ THE BOOK

SET PURPOSE Have children set a purpose for reading. Ask them how a community of insects is like a community of people.

COMPREHENSION QUESTIONS

PAGE 3 Why do you think many people are working together to build this home? *(Possible response: The work gets done much faster when people work together.)*

PAGES 5–6 What is the same about the pictures on these two pages? What is different? *(Both show a community eating together. But people take food and put it on a plate. Ants have the same piece of food.)*

PAGE 8 This picture shows ants working together to carry leaves and food. Why do you think they work together? *(It is too much work for one ant to do alone.)*

TEXT-TO-TEXT QUESTION

What other stories do you remember in which animals or people work together?

REVISIT THE BOOK

THINK AND SHARE
Answers
1. Possible response: a community, because everyone pitches in and helps in a special way. Many people working together get a job done more quickly than one person.
2. Possible responses: playground builder—set up slide, plant flowers, dig holes; ant—carry leaves, pile sand
3. Answers will vary but should reflect knowledge of the word *industrious*.

EXTEND UNDERSTANDING Have children think about other insects they know that might work together as a community.

RESPONSE OPTIONS

DRAMA Have children imagine they are tiny ants who must carry heavy leaves and food back to their homes. Have children think of props they can use to simulate leaves and food—pillows or boxes, perhaps, as leaves and food. They can "act out" an ant's journey.

SCIENCE CONNECTION

Weather permitting, have children go outdoors to observe ants busy at work. Provide magnifying glasses, and ask children to discuss what they see. If this is not possible, display picture books about ants in nature or in an ant farm. Ask children to point out the jobs ants do to help the community.

GRAPHIC ORGANIZER, PAGE 44

Have children complete the chart to show what both people and ants do together in their communities. Children can draw simple pictures or write words to fill in the chart. *(Responses: build, eat, work)*

Name_____

Fill in the chart to show how ants and people are alike.

What Ants and People Do

Gardens Change

SUMMARY Children read about the changes that take place in a garden by following the growing process of pumpkins.

VOCABULARY
High-Frequency Words
the

Concept Words

| garden | snow | seeds |
| leaves | flowers | pumpkins |

INTRODUCE THE BOOK

BUILD BACKGROUND Invite children to share their knowledge about gardens. If any have helped plant a garden at home, ask them to share about the changes they saw in the garden as it grew.

ELL Have children suggest words for things they find in the garden in English and in their home language. Provide a three-column chart. Help them write the English word in the first column, write the word in their home language in the second, and draw a picture in the third.

PREVIEW Invite children to take a picture walk to preview the text and illustrations. Discuss the changes taking place in the garden on each page.

READ THE BOOK

SET PURPOSE Have children set a purpose for reading *Gardens Change*. Ask them to think about all the things needed for the garden to grow well.

COMPREHENSION QUESTIONS

PAGE 3 Why is there snow on the ground on this page? *(It is winter.)*

PAGE 5 What has happened to the seeds that were planted? *(They grew leaves.)*

PAGE 7 How has the garden changed in this picture? *(Possible responses: The flowers are gone; the seeds have grown into pumpkins; the pumpkins are ready to be picked.)*

TEXT-TO-SELF QUESTION

What have you made using a pumpkin grown in a garden? *(Possible responses: jack-o-lantern, pumpkin pie)*

REVISIT THE BOOK

THINK AND SHARE
Answers
1. Seeds were planted, pumpkins grew, and then they were picked.
2. in the fall, around Halloween
3. Gardens grow and then die. Responses will vary for the second question based on the places children choose to talk about. They should demonstrate understanding that places can look very different over time.

EXTEND UNDERSTANDING Have children think about other things that grow in a garden. Make a list of their suggestions.

RESPONSE OPTIONS

ART Create a mural on a large sheet of butcher paper. Have children draw various plants and animals that can be found in a garden. Help children label each picture.

SCIENCE CONNECTION

Plant seeds in an egg carton to demonstrate planting and growing a garden. Talk through the stages of planting a garden, such as the importance of soil, sunlight, and so on. Try to use seeds rather than starter plants. Keep the "garden" near a window as a class garden, and teach children how to care for it.

GRAPHIC ORGANIZER, PAGE 46
Have children fill in the chart with drawings to show how the garden and pumpkin plants change throughout the year. *(Children's drawings should show the various stages of the garden.)*

Name_____

Fill in the chart to show how a pumpkin garden changes.

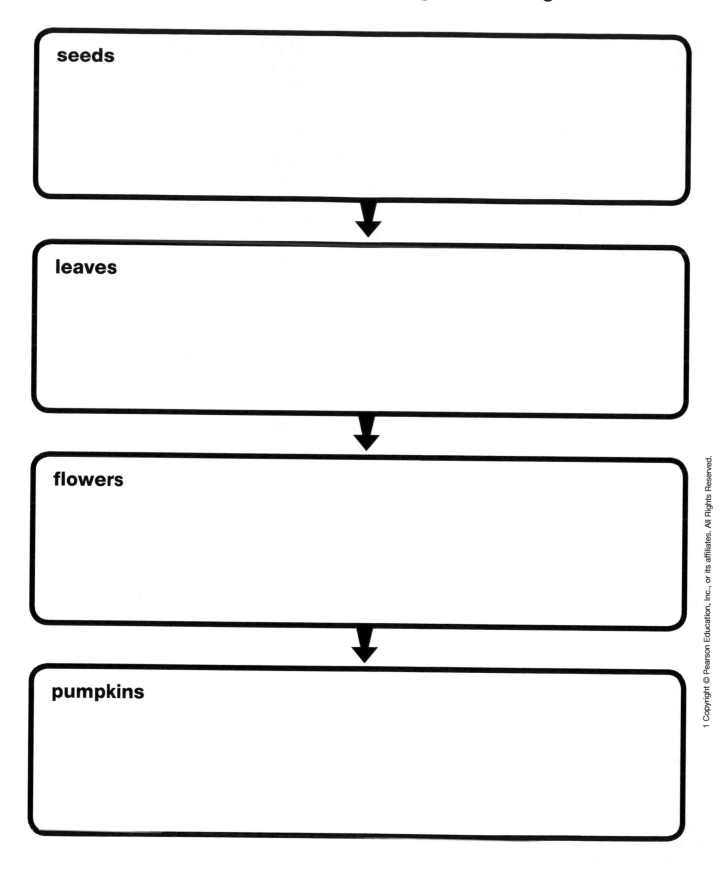

seeds

leaves

flowers

pumpkins

I Can Read

SUMMARY Children read about a boy who can read more as he learns more about reading.

VOCABULARY
High-Frequency Words
I   this

Concept Words
read   name   letter
word   sentence   page
book

INTRODUCE THE BOOK

BUILD BACKGROUND Invite children to share their reading experiences and successes. Ask children to share information about how they have grown as readers.

ELL Discuss words that relate to reading, particularly the concept words. Provide children with two sets of notecards. Write the English words on one set. On another set, have the children write the words in their home language or draw pictures of the word. Allow children to play a matching game with the cards.

PREVIEW Invite children to take a picture walk to preview the text and illustrations. Have children describe what the main character is doing on each page.

READ THE BOOK

SET PURPOSE Have children set a purpose for reading *I Can Read*. Ask children why it is important to learn to read.

COMPREHENSION QUESTIONS

PAGE 3 What is the main character pointing at? *(His name, Jim)*

PAGE 6 Do you think Jim enjoys reading? Why do you think that ? *(Possible responses: yes; He's smiling; he's sharing with a friend; he looks like he's having fun.)*

PAGE 7 Do you ever read with your friends? What books do you read together? *(Responses will vary.)*

TEXT-TO-SELF QUESTION
What is the best part of reading? What is the hardest part of reading? What do you like to read?

REVISIT THE BOOK
THINK AND SHARE
Answers
1. He's learning to read.
2. Possible responses: I'm learning to read; I can read a letter, word, sentence, and so on; I think reading is fun too.
3. Possible responses: He's proud of himself; he likes to read; he liked the book.

EXTEND UNDERSTANDING Ask children for examples of letters and words. Ask why knowing these can help them learn to read.

RESPONSE OPTIONS
WRITING Provide children with construction paper, markers, and crayons. Have them write the alphabet or words they know all over the paper in many colors.

SOCIAL STUDIES CONNECTION

Create a Picture Sort wall. Make letter cards for each letter of the alphabet (upper- and lower-case), and post them alphabetically across the wall. Give children several blank cards, and have them draw an object, allowing only one object per card. Help children label their objects, and have them tape their card below the letter the object name begins with. A theme may be used, such as Things in the Classroom or Things in Your House.

GRAPHIC ORGANIZER, PAGE 48
Have children fill in the web to show what they can read. Children may write words or provide examples. *(Possible responses: Mm, fun, Joel, I am happy.)*

Name_____

Fill in the web to show what we can read.

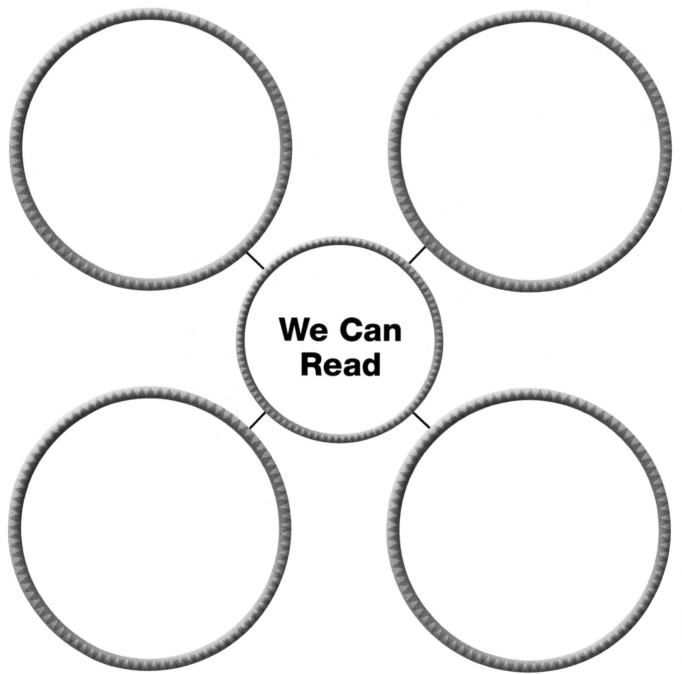

We Can
Read

Animals Change

SUMMARY Children read and learn that baby animals don't always look like the adults they grow into.

VOCABULARY

High-Frequency Words
a

Concept Words

baby	frog	change
snake	lion	bear
bird		

INTRODUCE THE BOOK

BUILD BACKGROUND Invite children to share what they know about animals that change as they grow. If they have pets at home, let them talk about what they have observed.

ELL Have children make a three-column list of animal names: one column for the word in English, one column for the word in their home language, and one column for them to draw the animal.

PREVIEW Invite children to take a picture walk of the reader. Have them describe and discuss the animals in the photos on each page. Ask children whether the baby is still the same animal if it looks different as an adult.

READ THE BOOK

SET PURPOSE Have children set a purpose for reading *Animals Change*. Ask them to think about growing up and the changes that might happen to them as they grow.

COMPREHENSION QUESTIONS

PAGE 3 How did the frog change from when it was a baby? (*It lost its tail.*)

PAGE 5 How does this snake change as it grows up? (*It gets longer and thicker.*)

PAGE 7 What is the baby bird doing to grow bigger and stronger? What does it need to grow? (*It is eating; it needs food.*)

TEXT-TO SELF QUESTIONS

These animals need things to help them grow bigger and stronger. What do they need? What do you need to grow up?

REVISIT THE BOOK

THINK AND SHARE
Answers
1. Possible response: The frog loses its tail.
2. Bigger: polar bear, lion, dog; Smaller: frog, snake, bird, dog.
3. Both get bigger, stronger, and look different.

EXTEND UNDERSTANDING Have children think of other animals that might change or look different as they grow up. Make a list of the children's ideas.

RESPONSE OPTIONS

WRITING Have children create more pages that might belong in this book. Have them draw the baby and adult versions of the animal, and help them write a sentence to match their picture, such as A baby cat will change.

SCIENCE CONNECTION

Provide nonfiction books that show other animals that change as they grow. Have children choose three animals that they think change the most, illustrate them, and create a wall collage with the pictures.

GRAPHIC ORGANIZER, PAGE 50

Work with children to fill in the chart to show how animals change. Have children draw a picture of each matching adult animal. (*Children's drawings should be a larger version of the baby animal shown.*)

Name_____

Fill in the chart to show how animals change.

Animals Change

Baby	Adult

Changes in the Garden

SUMMARY Children read about the changes that take place in plants throughout the growing process.

VOCABULARY
Concept Words

seeds	change	plants
fruits	vegetables	trees

INTRODUCE THE BOOK

BUILD BACKGROUND Invite children to share their knowledge about how plants change. If they have planted a garden or have a garden at home, ask them to share what they know about the way plants change as they grow.

ELL Have children suggest words for things they may find in the garden in English as well as in their home language. Write the English words on one set of blank cards. On another set, have children write the words in their home language or draw pictures of the words. Allow children to play a matching game with the cards.

PREVIEW Invite children to take a picture walk to preview the text and illustrations. Discuss what change is happening in the garden on each page.

READ THE BOOK

SET PURPOSE Have children set a purpose for reading *Changes in the Garden.* Ask them to think about the many ways plants can change as they grow.

COMPREHENSION QUESTIONS

PAGE 4 How did the plant at the top of this page change? *(It grew more leaves, grew bigger, got thicker.)*

PAGE 5 How is the flower in the bottom picture different from the flower in the top picture? *(It is open.)*

PAGE 8 Why do you think this tree changes? *(It changes from summer to winter; its leaves fall off.)*

TEXT-TO-TEXT QUESTION

What other books about "change" have you read? What were the books about?

REVISIT THE BOOK

THINK AND SHARE
Answers
1. Possible responses: They grow out of the ground; they grow roots, stems, leaves; they get bigger.
2. Possible responses: tomatoes, corn, carrots, flowers, bushes, plants
3. Responses will vary according to the season.

EXTEND UNDERSTANDING Have children think about other things in nature that change. Make a list of the suggestions. *(forests, ponds, lakes, fields, animals)*

RESPONSE OPTIONS

ART Have children draw or paint a picture of what a garden would look like in the summer and another picture of the same garden in the fall or winter. Help them write a caption for each picture.

SOCIAL STUDIES CONNECTION
Provide old nature magazines for children to look through. Have children find two or three things in nature that they think change the most, encourage them to share why they think so with classmates, and then have them cut and paste their finds onto construction paper. Gather and bind all pages to create a class book.

GRAPHIC ORGANIZER, PAGE 52
Help children fill in the web with things that change in the garden. Children may draw pictures and/or write words. *(Possible responses: any vegetable, fruit, seed, or flower)*

Name_____

Fill in the web to show what changes in a garden.

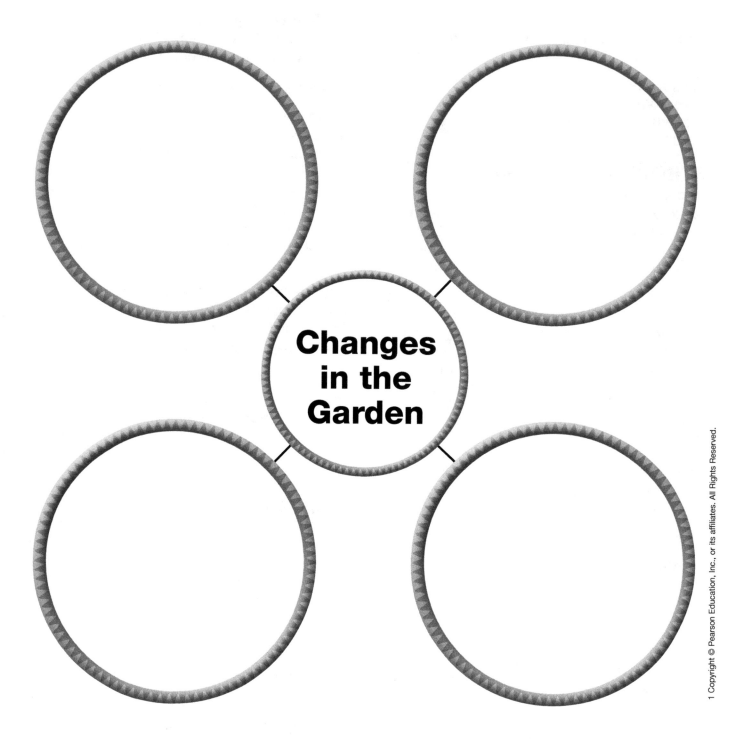

Changes
in the
Garden

52

Caterpillars Change

SUMMARY Children read about the changes a caterpillar goes through as it becomes a butterfly.

VOCABULARY

High-Frequency Words

this	a
an	of

Concept Words

leaf	egg	caterpillar
cocoon	butterfly	

INTRODUCE THE BOOK

BUILD BACKGROUND Invite children to share their knowledge about caterpillars.

ELL Have children suggest words for the metamorphosis in English as well as in their home language. Make a list of their suggestions, and help them with any words they don't know.

PREVIEW Invite children to take a picture walk to preview the text and illustrations. Discuss what is happening on each page.

READ THE BOOK

SET PURPOSE Have children set a purpose for reading *Caterpillars Change*. Ask them to think about why a caterpillar changes throughout its life.

COMPREHENSION QUESTIONS

PAGE 3 Why is this leaf important to the caterpillar? *(It's where the egg is laid; the caterpillar can eat it as food to grow.)*

PAGE 4 Describe what you see on this page. *(leaf; egg; small egg; sky/clouds; green leaf; white egg; leaf hair)*

PAGE 6 Why do you think the caterpillar makes a cocoon? *(to grow; to sleep; to be safe while it grows)*

TEXT-TO-SELF QUESTION

How are you similar to this caterpillar? How are you different?

REVISIT THE BOOK

THINK AND SHARE
Answers
1. Possible responses: Yes. It was pretty; it flew around; it landed on flowers, it was colorful.
2. Four changes: egg, caterpillar *(larva),* cocoon *(pupa),* butterfly *(adult)*
3. Possible responses: frogs, flies, moths, mealworms, ants

EXTEND UNDERSTANDING Discuss other animals or insects that may change or look different to survive. Try to have examples from magazines to show the children.

RESPONSE OPTIONS
DRAMA Have children role play the stages of a caterpillar's life cycle. Children can curl up for the egg stage; wriggle around for the caterpillar stage; wrap their arms around themselves and pretend to sleep for the cocoon stage; and finally act out the emergence from the cocoon as butterflies.

SCIENCE CONNECTION

On a large sheet of butcher paper, draw the four stages of the metamorphosis (egg, caterpillar, cocoon, butterfly) clockwise in the stated order with an arrow pointing to the next stage. There should also be an arrow pointing from the "butterfly" stage to the "egg" stage. Have children discuss the importance of the stages to a caterpillar, and write their suggestions near the appropriate stage. Be sure to include how the physical characteristics of each stage are important to the butterfly's survival.

GRAPHIC ORGANIZER, PAGE 54
Help children fill in the cycle chart with the stages of a butterfly's metamorphosis. Children may draw pictures and/or write words. *(egg, caterpillar, cocoon, butterfly)*

Name_____

Fill in the chart to show how a caterpillar changes.

How a Caterpillar Changes

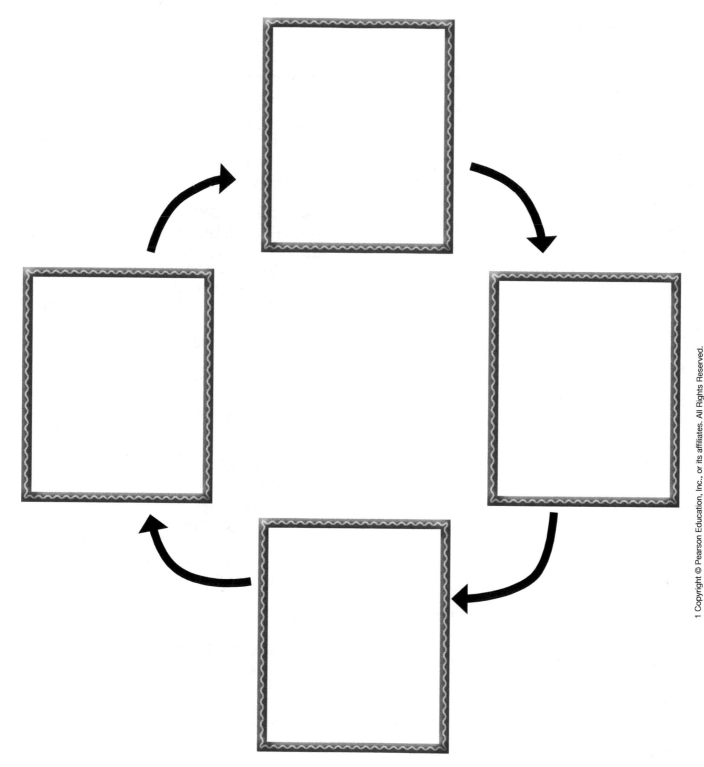

In the Winter

SUMMARY Children read about the various activities animals do to survive the winter.

VOCABULARY

High-Frequency Words
  this

Concept Words

animal	sleeps	hides
flies	digs	eats
huddles		

INTRODUCE THE BOOK

BUILD BACKGROUND Invite children to share their knowledge about animals during the winter. If they have noticed changes in animal behavior in the winter, ask them to share their observations.

ELL Pair less proficient English-speaking children with proficient English-speaking classmates. Have them discuss the activities the animals in the book do during the winter, and allow them to act out the activities.

PREVIEW Invite children to take a picture walk to preview the text and illustrations. Discuss how the animal on each page changed its behavior for the winter.

READ THE BOOK

SET PURPOSE Have children set a purpose for reading *In the Winter*. Ask them to think about why the animals need to do what they do.

COMPREHENSION QUESTIONS

PAGE 3 What is this animal doing? *(sleeping)* Why? *(to stay warm; to eat less)*

PAGE 5 Where do you think these birds are going? *(someplace warm; south)*

PAGE 7 How does eating help this animal stay warm? *(Eating makes it fatter; it makes its fur thicker.)*

TEXT-TO-SELF QUESTION

Which of these activities makes you the warmest?

REVISIT THE BOOK

THINK AND SHARE
Answers

1. Possible responses: sleep, huddle, hide, dig, eat, fly south
2. Possible responses: wear thick clothes, and stay inside where it's heated. Animals don't wear clothes, and their homes aren't heated.
3. Possible responses: to stay warm; to stay alive

EXTEND UNDERSTANDING Have children discuss more activities other animals might do to survive the winter. Make a list of the suggestions.

RESPONSE OPTIONS

DRAMA Have children act out an animal and the activity it does to stay warm in the winter. Allow classmates to guess the animal and the activity being pantomimed.

SCIENCE CONNECTION

Provide science photo books about animals during the winter (can include fish, reptiles, insects). Have children choose two creatures they think change the most during the winter. Help children write a sentence or two explaining how the animal changes and why they chose it. Encourage children to illustrate their choices.

GRAPHIC ORGANIZER, PAGE 56

Help children fill in the web with the activities animals do in the winter. Children can draw pictures and/or write words. *(Possible responses: sleep, hide, fly, dig, eat, huddle)*

Name_____

Fill in the web to show what animals do in the winter.

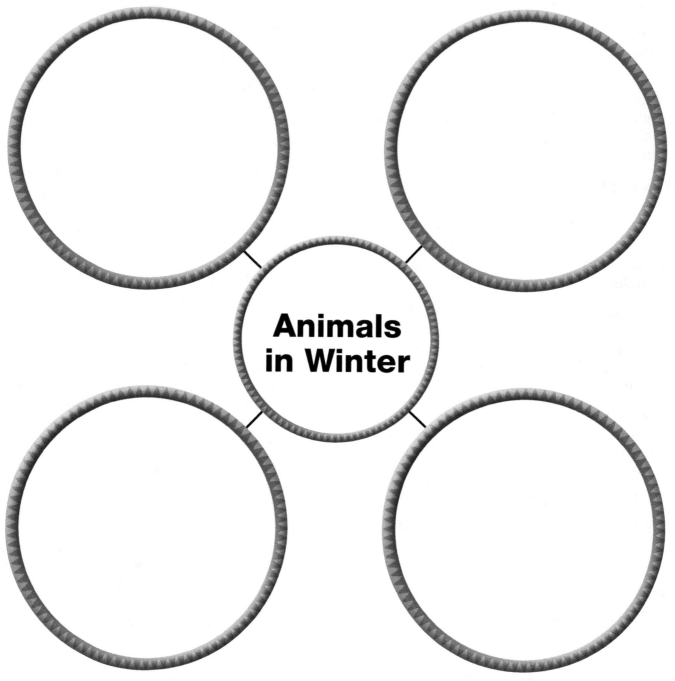

Animals
in Winter

56

Surprise, Surprise!

SUMMARY Children read about the various surprises other children receive.

VOCABULARY
High-Frequency Words

a	was	some

Concept Words

surprise	party	puppy
blue ribbon	flowers	rainy day
hug		

INTRODUCE THE BOOK

BUILD BACKGROUND Invite children to talk about a time when they were surprised. If they helped to surprise someone else, allow them to share what they did.

ELL Have children write the concept words in English on one side of a blank card. On the other side, have children write the same words in their home language or draw pictures of the word. Use the cards for practice.

PREVIEW Invite children to take a picture walk to preview the text and illustrations. Discuss the surprise shown on each page.

READ THE BOOK

SET PURPOSE Have children set a purpose for reading *Surprise, Surprise!* Discuss why people might like to be surprised.

COMPREHENSION QUESTIONS

PAGE 3 What is happening in this picture? (*Possible responses: Tim had a surprise party; he's blowing out candles; it's Tim's birthday.*)

PAGE 5 Why do you think the blue ribbon was a surprise to Pat? (*Possible response: He didn't know he would win.*)

PAGE 7 Is a rainy day a good surprise or a bad surprise? Why do you think that? (*Possible responses: Good: It's fun to play in the rain; it's good for plants; it cools us on a hot day. Bad: It can ruin your plans; it can cause flooding; it's cold.*)

TEXT-TO-SELF QUESTION
Do you like surprises? What kinds of surprises do you like? What kinds of surprises don't you like? Why?

REVISIT THE BOOK
THINK AND SHARE
Answers
1. Responses will vary.
2. Responses will vary.
3. Responses will vary, but should be supported with examples.

EXTEND UNDERSTANDING Discuss why the surprise on each page is a valuable treasure. (*Possible responses: Party: good friends, presents; Puppy: new friend, can care for it; Blue ribbon: rewards hard work, builds self-confidence; and so on.*)

RESPONSE OPTIONS
WRITING Have children choose one surprise from the book and pretend they are the child on the page. As that person, have children write a thank-you card to the person who gave them the surprise. Encourage children to illustrate their cards.

SOCIAL STUDIES CONNECTION
Have children draw a picture of a special surprise they received. Post a picture of a large treasure chest on a bulletin board with children's treasured surprises flowing out of it.

GRAPHIC ORGANIZER, PAGE 58
Have children fill in the main idea chart to show surprises that can be treasures. Children may draw pictures and/or write words. (*Possible responses: a party, a puppy, a blue ribbon, flowers, a rainy day, a hug*)

Name_____

Fill in the chart to show surprises that can be treasures.

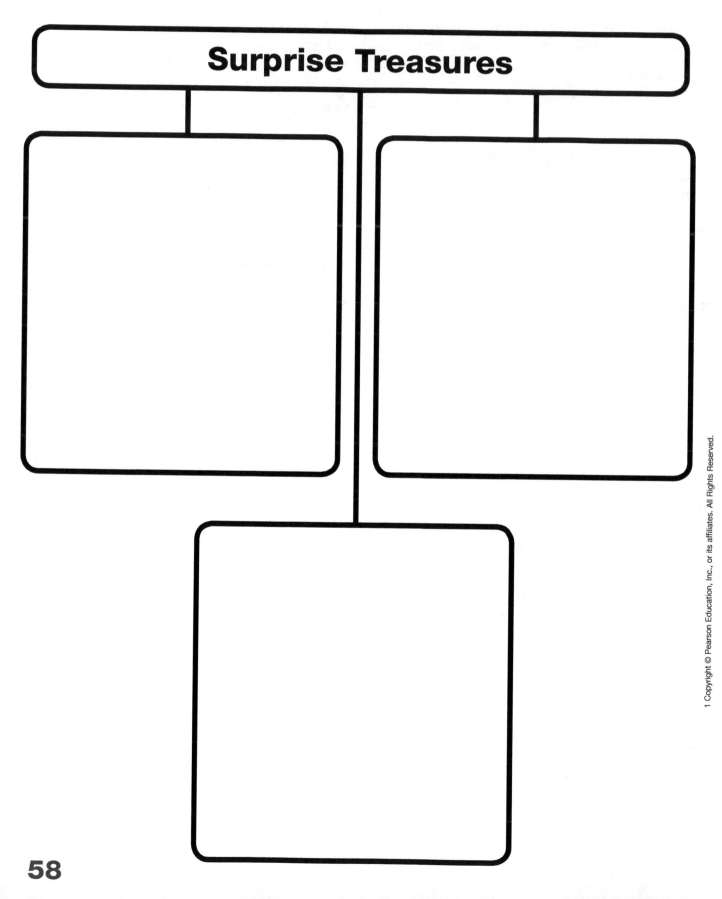

Surprise Treasures

Special Stories

SUMMARY Children read about many kinds of stories that are special in different ways.

VOCABULARY

High-Frequency Words

I a

Concept Words

story	funny	scary
surprising	exciting	sad
interesting		

INTRODUCE THE BOOK

BUILD BACKGROUND Invite children to tell about favorite stories that they think are special. Encourage them to explain whether the stories are scary, funny, interesting, and so on.

ELL Help children understand the English concept words they are not familiar with. Have them tell a classmate the word in their home language. As a class, have children act out each emotion word.

PREVIEW Invite children to take a picture walk to preview the text and illustrations. Have children discuss what might be happening in the story the child is reading that would cause each reaction.

READ THE BOOK

SET PURPOSE Have children set a purpose for reading *Special Stories*. Ask them to think about why the child on each page might enjoy reading that type of story.

COMPREHENSION QUESTIONS

PAGE 3 Describe what is happening in this photo. *(Possible responses: The girl is reading a funny story; she is laughing; she is smiling.)*

PAGE 4 Why do you think the boy is under a blanket? *(Possible responses: He's scared; the story is scaring him; he feels safe there.)*

PAGE 7 What makes a story sad? *(Possible responses: when something bad happens; when a pet runs away; when your best friend moves away)*

TEXT-TO-SELF QUESTION

Which of these types of books do you like to read? Why?

REVISIT THE BOOK

THINK AND SHARE

Answers

1. funny, scary, surprising, exciting, sad, interesting
2. Responses will vary.
3. Responses will vary but should demonstrate knowledge of the word *treasure,* and children should support their answers with reasons.

EXTEND UNDERSTANDING Ask children to think about their favorite story. Have them illustrate the story, and help them write a sentence or two to go with their illustrations.

RESPONSE OPTIONS

DRAMA In groups, have children choose a story they all enjoy. Then allow them to act out the story for the entire class.

SOCIAL STUDIES CONNECTION

Provide well-illustrated picture books from various cultures and allow children to look through them. Have children choose their favorite book and then create an illustration and a sentence to tell about it. Collect the pages to create a class book.

GRAPHIC ORGANIZER, PAGE 60

Have children fill in the web with types of stories that can be treasures. Children may draw pictures and/or write words. *(Possible responses: funny, scary, surprising, exciting, sad, interesting)*

Name _____

Fill in the web with kinds of stories that are treasures.

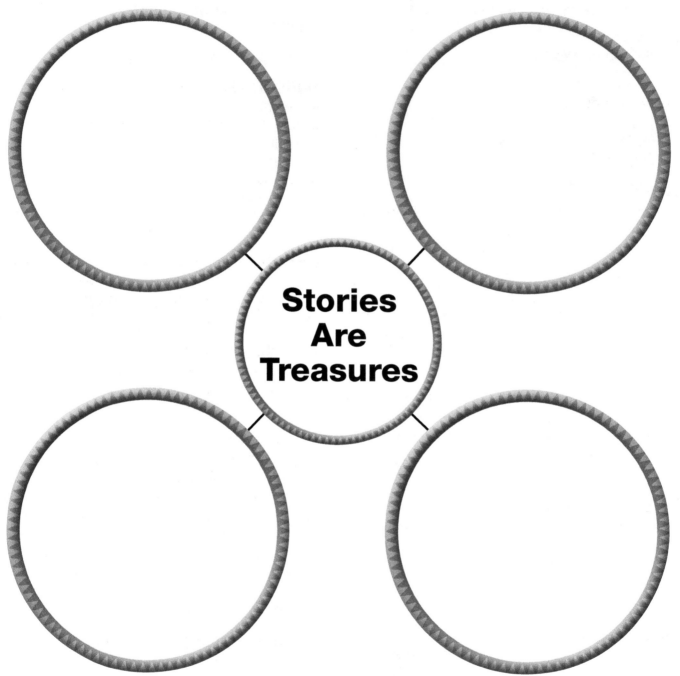

Our Country's Treasures

SUMMARY Children read about some of the treasures that there are to see in the United States.

VOCABULARY
High-Frequency Words
a   the

Concept Words
building   treasure   visit
canyon   mountain   waterfall
bridge   forest

INTRODUCE THE BOOK

BUILD BACKGROUND Invite children to tell about a vacation they may have taken in the United States or any historic places they have visited.

ELL Using a large picture book of famous monuments or historic sites in the United States, have children suggest words in their home language that describe these places. Help children with the same words in English.

PREVIEW Invite children to take a picture walk to preview the text and illustrations. Discuss the national treasure that is pictured on each page.

READ THE BOOK

SET PURPOSE Have children set a purpose for reading *Our Country's Treasures*. Ask them to think about why each place is a treasure.

COMPREHENSION QUESTIONS

PAGE 3 Why do you think this building is a treasure? *(Possible response: It's where our President lives.)*

PAGE 5 What do you see in this picture? *(men, faces, heads)* Who are the men carved on the mountain? *(Possible responses: presidents, Washington, Jefferson, Roosevelt, Lincoln)*

PAGE 7 How is this bridge a different kind of treasure from the waterfall on page 6? How are they the same? *(One is found in nature, the other is man-made. They are both special places.)*

TEXT-TO-TEXT QUESTION
What other books or stories about treasures have you read? Tell about them.

REVISIT THE BOOK
THINK AND SHARE
Answers
1. People: White House, Mount Rushmore, Golden Gate Bridge; Nature: Grand Canyon, Niagara Falls, Redwood Forest
2. They are special, valuable, and/or historical to the country.
3. Responses will vary but should be supported by reasons.

EXTEND UNDERSTANDING Have children suggest other treasures in our country. Make a list of the suggestions on the board.

RESPONSE OPTIONS

ART Have children choose a place from the book and create a postcard to a friend or relative from that place. Have them draw a picture on one side of a large postcard-sized paper and write a short message on the other.

SOCIAL STUDIES CONNECTION

Provide books with photos of various treasures in the United States. Have children choose one or two treasures they think are important. Encourage them to share the reasons for their choice. Have children draw a picture of themselves at the treasured location, and help them write a sentence or two explaining why it is a national treasure.

GRAPHIC ORGANIZER, PAGE 62
Have children complete the web to show treasures in our country. Children may draw pictures and/or write words for the treasures they have read about or any others they know of.

Name_____

Fill in the web with treasures in our country.

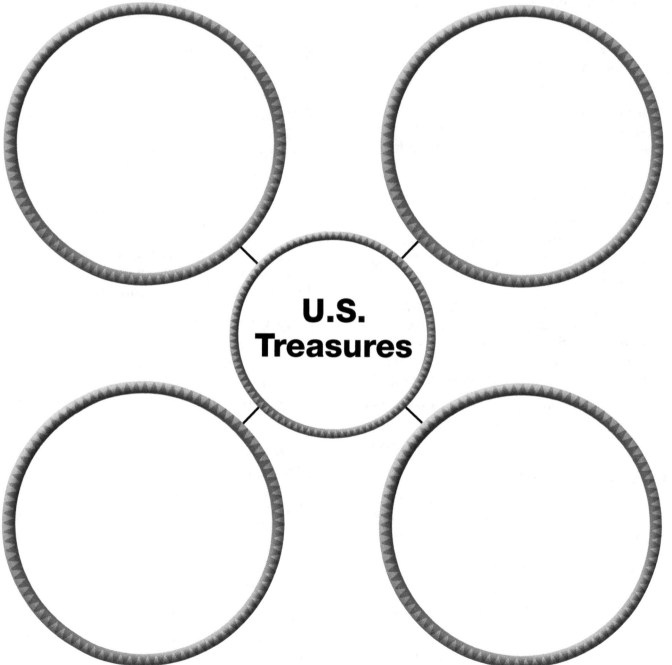

U.S.
Treasures

Places We Treasure

SUMMARY Children read about various places that might be called treasures and what they might see there.

VOCABULARY
High-Frequency Words

this	is	a
we	see	here

Concept Words

ranch	treasure	farm
lake	lighthouse	beach
house		

INTRODUCE THE BOOK

BUILD BACKGROUND Ask: What does it mean to treasure something? Invite children to tell about a place they know about or have visited that they treasure.

ELL Have children suggest words for things they might see at the locations in the book. Write the suggestions on the board in English and in their home language. Help children with words they do not know.

PREVIEW Invite children to take a picture walk to preview the text and illustrations. Discuss what they see on each page.

READ THE BOOK

SET PURPOSE Have children set a purpose for reading *Places We Treasure*. Ask them to think about what makes each place a treasure.

COMPREHENSION QUESTIONS

PAGE 3 What do you see in this picture? *(horses, fences, trees, mountains, sky, and so on.)* Why would this place be a treasure? *(Possible response: It's beautiful; it has fresh air.)*

PAGE 6 For whom do you think this lighthouse is a treasure? *(for sailors, for the people who live nearby, for us to visit and enjoy)*

PAGE 8 Why is this house a treasure? *(Possible response: It's Grandpa's house.)*

TEXT-TO-SELF QUESTION
What place is a treasure to you? Why?

REVISIT THE BOOK
THINK AND SHARE
Answers
1. something that is valuable to you
2. Possible responses: They're pretty; they're places we can enjoy visiting; they make us happy; they're special to us; we have good memories there.
3. Responses will vary but should be supported with reasons.

EXTEND UNDERSTANDING Have children discuss things they, their families, or their friends may treasure that others do not. Have children illustrate and label these treasures.

RESPONSE OPTIONS
WRITING Have children choose one of the treasured places in the book. Help them write a sentence or two explaining what makes that place a treasure. Encourage them to illustrate their responses.

SOCIAL STUDIES CONNECTION

Provide old magazines and have children find pictures of objects in their rooms or around their homes that they treasure. Have children cut out these items and paste them onto a sheet of construction paper. Help children label the treasures.

GRAPHIC ORGANIZER, PAGE 64
Have children compete the pictograph to show who might treasure each of these special places. Children can draw pictures and/or write words. *(Possible responses: ranch: cowboy; farm: farmer; lake: fisherman; lighthouse: boater; beach: vacationer; house: boy or girl)*

Name_____

Fill in the chart to show who treasures these places.

Place	Who Treasures It?

Treasures We Share

SUMMARY Children read about special things children share with others.

VOCABULARY

High-Frequency Words

we	are
they	too

Concept Words

share	movies	treasures
stories	pictures	rocking chairs
watches	happy times	

INTRODUCE THE BOOK

BUILD BACKGROUND Discuss with children how sharing a special object or a special time with family can be a treasure. Remind them that doing things with others is often more fun than doing them alone.

ELL Have children suggest words for things they do with their families. List the words on the board in English and in their home language.

PREVIEW Invite children to take a picture walk to preview the text and illustrations. Discuss the treasure on each page, whose treasure it is, and with whom they are sharing it.

READ THE BOOK

SET PURPOSE Have children set a purpose for reading *Treasures We Share*. Ask them to think about why the people in the book might want to share their treasure with another person.

COMPREHENSION QUESTIONS

PAGE 3 How is watching a movie a treasure? *(It is time you spend together with the people you love.)*

PAGE 5 Is the painting on this page an expensive one? *(No.)* Then why is it a treasure? *(It was made for someone special.)*

PAGE 7 Why is this watch a treasure? *(Possible response: It's been passed down through the family; it's special to the family.)*

TEXT-TO-SELF QUESTION

Which treasure in this book is a treasure to your family too? What other treasures do you share?

REVISIT THE BOOK

THINK AND SHARE

Answers

1. something special you share with your family; can be time spent together or an heirloom.
2. Responses will vary but should be supported with reasons.
3. Responses will vary but should reflect an appropriate treasure.

EXTEND UNDERSTANDING Have children think about other things that families might treasure. List the suggestions on the board.

RESPONSE OPTIONS

WRITING Have children write about a treasure they have shared and with whom they shared it. Encourage children to illustrate their sentences and create a book of class treasures.

SOCIAL STUDIES CONNECTION

Create a treasure hunt for children with old magazines. Provide a list of search words on the board—objects families might treasure *(a vase, a piece of artwork, a ring),* and have children cut out the best example they can find of each item and paste them onto a sheet of construction paper. Have them label the collage Family Treasures.

GRAPHIC ORGANIZER, PAGE 66

Have children complete the web to show special times or treasures they like to share. Responses will vary but could include examples from the book or others children suggest.

Name_____

Fill in the web to show treasures you share.

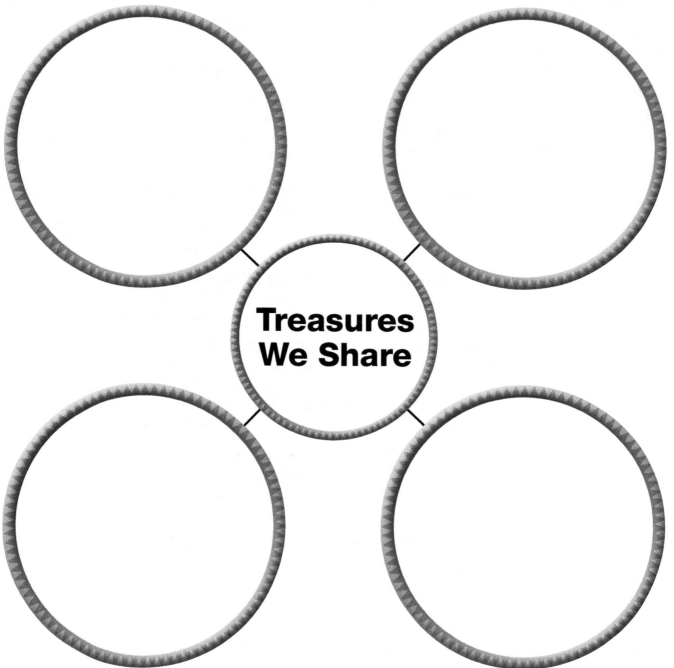

**Treasures
We Share**

66

My Town

SUMMARY Students read about the various activities children can share with neighbors in their town.

VOCABULARY
High-Frequency Words

my	a	together

Concept Words

town	playground	field
pool	parades	fairs
neighbors		

INTRODUCE THE BOOK

BUILD BACKGROUND Invite children to tell about activities they have shared with their neighbors.

ELL Show the pictures from the book. Have children act out the activity shown on each page. Make a list of the activities on the board in English and in their home languages.

PREVIEW Invite children to take a picture walk to preview the text and illustrations. Discuss the activities taking place on each page.

READ THE BOOK

SET PURPOSE Have children set a purpose for reading *My Town*. Ask them to think about why a town might provide these activities for neighbors.

COMPREHENSION QUESTIONS

PAGE 3 Why is a playground a treasure? *(It is a place where kids get together to have fun; it's a place to make friends.)*

PAGE 4-5 Why does a town provide areas such as a field and a pool for its townspeople? *(in order to build the sense of community; to have a place we can share together and a place to have fun together)*

PAGE 8 Why is important to have friends and neighbors to treasure things with? *(It makes you happier; you're not alone or lonely.)*

TEXT-TO-SELF QUESTION
With whom do you most like to do things in your town? Why?

REVISIT THE BOOK

THINK AND SHARE
Answers
1. Responses will vary.
2. Responses will vary.
3. Responses will vary but should be supported with reasons.

EXTEND UNDERSTANDING Explain to children that we often depend on neighbors in an emergency. Discuss the importance of developing friendships with neighbors. Ask them to suggest times when we might need our neighbors for help in an emergency.

RESPONSE OPTIONS

ART Have children draw pictures of a favorite activity they do with their neighbors. Help them write a sentence or two explaining why they like it.

SOCIAL STUDIES CONNECTION
Have children create a mural of their town. Help them locate and label places where town activities are held. Display the map in your classroom.

GRAPHIC ORGANIZER, PAGE 68
Have children complete the chart to show activities that they can share with neighbors in their town. They can draw pictures or write words. *(Possible responses: climb, play, swim, march, eat, have fun)*

Name_____

Fill in the chart to show what we do with neighbors.

Things to Do with Neighbors

Great Ideas

SUMMARY Children read about inventions that started as great ideas and how they help us.

VOCABULARY
High-Frequency Words

the	were
a	us

Concept Words

idea	light bulbs	cars
gloves	telephones	computers
playgrounds		

INTRODUCE THE BOOK

BUILD BACKGROUND Invite children to talk about an invention they think was a great idea and why they think that.

ELL Write the concept words on the board and read them aloud with children. Have children choose one word and draw a picture of it. Then help children label their drawing with the word.

PREVIEW Invite children to take a picture walk to preview the text and photos in the book. Discuss the "great idea" shown on each page.

READ THE BOOK

SET PURPOSE Have children set a purpose for reading *Great Ideas*. Ask them to think about why having these great ideas is important.

COMPREHENSION QUESTIONS

PAGE 3 Who do you think this man is?
(Possible response: the man who invented the light bulb)

PAGE 6 Why do people use telephones?
(Possible responses: to talk to people; to call family or friends; to get help; to order a pizza)

PAGE 7 How do you use a computer to learn?
(Possible responses: by playing games; by searching the Internet)

TEXT-TO-SELF QUESTION
What great idea have you had?

REVISIT THE BOOK

THINK AND SHARE
Answers
1. Responses will vary but should be one of the inventions in the book.
2. Responses will vary, but children might suggest that a microwave helps people cook; a cell phone helps people talk wherever they are.
3. Responses will vary but should reflect thought about a problem that needs solving.

EXTEND UNDERSTANDING Have children think about other inventions around their house and why each was necessary or important. Make a list of the inventions on the board.

RESPONSE OPTIONS

ART Have children choose an invention or "great idea" from the board and draw a picture of it. Help children label their pictures with the name of the invention. Use the pictures to make a "great ideas" bulletin board.

SCIENCE CONNECTION

Display pictures of or the actual inventions, such as a cell phone, a hair dryer, an electric can opener, a hand-held can opener, a pad of sticky notes, a paper clip, or others. Have children name each invention and discuss how each makes life easier.

GRAPHIC ORGANIZER, PAGE 70
Help children complete the web with great ideas that help people. Children may draw pictures and/or write words to complete the chart. *(Possible responses: light bulb, car, gloves, telephone, computer, playground)*

Name_____

Fill in the web to show great ideas.

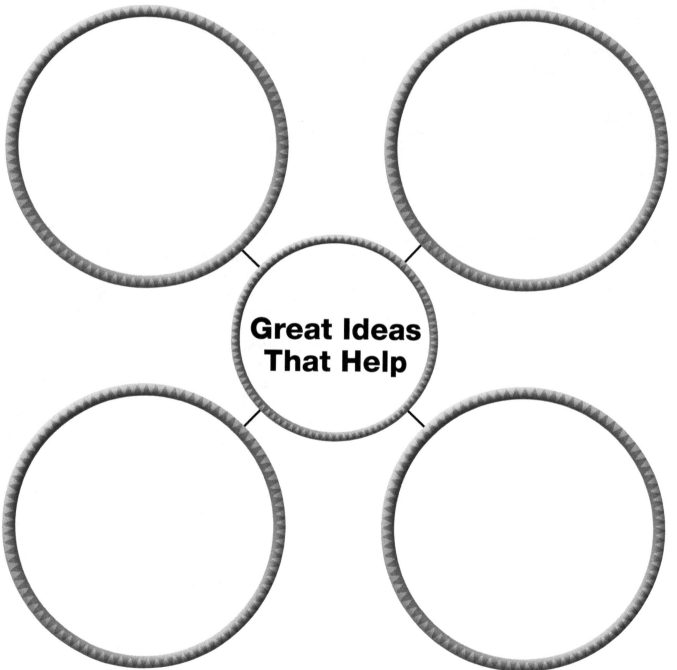

Great Ideas That Help

70

Ways We Learn

SUMMARY Children read about ways to learn new things.

VOCABULARY
High-Frequency Words

learn	by
what	doing

Concept Words

reading	listening	caring
building	helping	playing

INTRODUCE THE BOOK

BUILD BACKGROUND Ask children for examples of something new that they learned. Talk about how they learned it.

ELL Pair less proficient English-speaking children with proficient English-speaking classmates. Have them discuss ways people learn and allow them to act out these ways.

PREVIEW Invite children to take a picture walk to preview the text and photos. Discuss what the children are doing in each photo.

READ THE BOOK

SET PURPOSE Have children set a purpose for reading *Ways We Learn*. Ask them to think about why learning in different ways is helpful.

COMPREHENSION QUESTIONS

PAGE 5 How is Jon showing that he cares? *(Possible response: by playing with the puppy)*

PAGE 7 What are other ways to help besides drying dishes? *(Possible responses: setting the table; taking out the trash; sweeping the floor)*

PAGE 8 Why is Lin looking at the board? *(Possible response: because she is thinking about where to move her pieces)*

TEXT-TO-TEXT QUESTION

What other books or stories have you read in which someone learned something?

REVISIT THE BOOK

THINK AND SHARE
Answers

1. Responses will vary. Possible responses: I like learning to cook. I like learning to play baseball.
2. Responses will vary. Possible response: My friends like learning to play new games.
3. Responses will vary but should reflect a variety of ways to learn.

EXTEND UNDERSTANDING Invite children to think about people who can't see or hear and the ways they might learn new things. Explain what Braille is and how it is used as a tool for reading and learning.

RESPONSE OPTIONS

WRITING Have children write about one thing that they learned how to do recently. Then have them illustrate their response. Make a display of the responses.

SOCIAL STUDIES CONNECTION

Write the concept words on the board. Ask children to suggest places in the community where they can participate in each activity. Have children draw pictures of these places and then organize them under the correct concept words.

GRAPHIC ORGANIZER, PAGE 72

Have children complete the pictograph to tell various ways of learning. Children will write a sentence next to each picture to complete the graph. *(Responses: We learn by reading; We learn by listening; We learn by building; We learn by helping; We learn by playing.)*

Name_____

Fill in the graph to show how we learn.

How do we learn?

Who Likes the Oak Tree?

SUMMARY Children read about an oak tree and all the creatures that enjoy it.

VOCABULARY
High-Frequency Words

who	a
this	here

Concept Words

caterpillar	crawls	woodpecker
pecks	robin	builds
squirrel	owl	

INTRODUCE THE BOOK

BUILD BACKGROUND Invite children to share what they know about animals that live in trees. Ask them why these animals like trees.

ELL Have children suggest words for animals that live in trees in English as well as their home language. Make a list of their suggestions on the board and help children with any words they don't know.

PREVIEW Invite children to take a picture walk to preview the text and photos in the book. Discuss the living creatures shown on each page.

READ THE BOOK

SET PURPOSE Have children set a purpose for reading *Who Likes the Oak Tree?* Ask them to think about why it is important to have trees in a community.

COMPREHENSION QUESTIONS

PAGE 3 Where is the caterpillar crawling? *(on a leaf; in the oak tree)*

PAGE 7 Why is an oak tree important to an owl? *(Possible response: because it provides a home for the owl)*

PAGE 8 How can an oak tree be a place to play? *(Possible responses: We can hang a swing from a tree branch. We can climb the tree.)*

TEXT-TO-WORLD QUESTION
How are trees important to your community?

REVISIT THE BOOK
THINK AND SHARE
Answers
1. Possible responses: a caterpillar, a woodpecker, a robin, a squirrel, an owl, children.
2. Responses will vary but should include some aspect of a mystery or problem to solve.
3. Possible responses: look for clues; use the clues to make a guess; find the answer to a question.

EXTEND UNDERSTANDING Discuss why trees are important to some animals. Ask: Are all trees the same? How are they different?

RESPONSE OPTIONS
DRAMA Write the noun concept words on the board. Have children choose one and pantomime what this living thing does. Have classmates guess which living thing is being pantomimed.

SCIENCE CONNECTION
Supply leaves for children. Ask them to make observations about their leaf. Have children share what they observed. Help them write their observations and then glue the leaf to their paper.

GRAPHIC ORGANIZER, PAGE 74
Help children complete the chart to show what each animal does in the oak tree. Children may draw pictures and/or write words to complete the chart. *(caterpillar—crawls; woodpecker—pecks; robin—builds; squirrel—eats; owl—hides)*

Name_____

Finish the chart to tell what each animal does.

Who Likes the Oak Tree?

Simple Machines

SUMMARY Children read and learn about simple machines.

VOCABULARY
High-Frequency Words
this   a

Concept Words
machine   lever   wheel
axle   ramp   pulley
wedge

INTRODUCE THE BOOK

BUILD BACKGROUND Invite children to tell about simple machines they have used.

ELL Use the images in the book to show children examples of each concept word. Write the words on the board and read them together.

PREVIEW Invite children to take a picture walk to preview the text and photos in the book. Discuss the simple machine shown in each photo.

READ THE BOOK

SET PURPOSE Have children set a purpose for reading *Simple Machines*. Ask them to think about how simple machines help people everyday.

COMPREHENSION QUESTIONS

PAGE 3 What is the man using the lever for? *(to pry open the box)*

PAGE 6 How does a ramp make work easier? *(Possible response: It allows us to move heavy objects without lifting.)*

PAGE 7 Look carefully at the picture. How do you think a pulley works? *(Possible response: When you pull on one end of a rope, it moves on a wheel and lifts something attached to the other end.)*

TEXT-TO-TEXT QUESTION
Can you tell about any other books or stories that are about machines?

REVISIT THE BOOK
THINK AND SHARE
Answers
1. Possible responses: A wheel helps move a vehicle, such as a bike, a wagon, or a car; a wedge is used to split something apart.
2. Responses will vary but should mention a machine and be supported with examples.
3. Simple machines make it easier to move things from one place to another. They help us lift things and open things.

EXTEND UNDERSTANDING Explain to children that many small gadgets are really simple machines. For example, a bottle opener is a lever, a rolling pizza cutter is a wheel, and so on. Have children think of other examples.

RESPONSE OPTIONS
SPEAKING List the simple machines on the board. Have children sit in a circle. Then have them each choose one machine and tell one thing it can be used for.

SCIENCE CONNECTION
Provide photos of a variety of simple machines. Have children identify each machine.
Then have them discuss what the machine is doing and how it makes life easier.

GRAPHIC ORGANIZER, PAGE 76
Help children complete the web with the types of simple machines. Children will write words to complete the web. *(lever, wheel, axle, ramp, pulley, wedge)*

Name_____

Fill in the web to show simple machines.

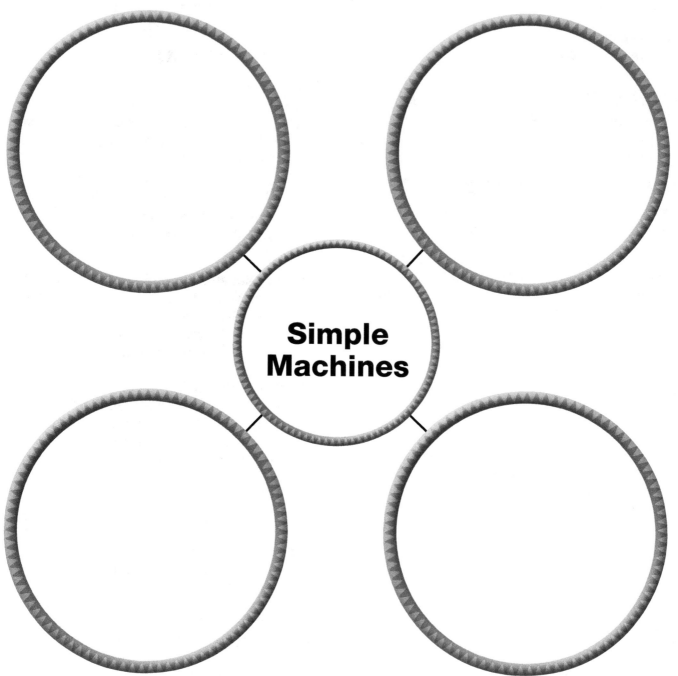

Simple Machines

76

Telephones Help Us Every Day

SUMMARY Children read about the people we talk to using telephones.

VOCABULARY
High-Frequency Words

we	to
the	friends

Concept Words

telephones	doctor	teacher
librarian	builder	vet

INTRODUCE THE BOOK

BUILD BACKGROUND Invite children to share their knowledge about using a telephone. Explain the steps taken to place a phone call.

ELL Write the concept words on the board and read them aloud with children. Then provide children with two sets of notecards. Write the English words on one set. On the other set, have children draw pictures of the words. Allow them to play a matching game with the cards.

PREVIEW Invite children to take a picture walk to preview the text and photos. Have children guess the career of the person on each page.

READ THE BOOK

SET PURPOSE Have children set a purpose for reading *Telephones Help Us Every Day*. Ask children why telephones are important.

COMPREHENSION QUESTIONS

PAGE 3 Why would it be important to use a telephone to talk to the doctor? *(Possible response: It's important to be able to reach the doctor in an emergency.)*

PAGE 6 Why might we need to talk to the builder? *(Possible response: to find out when our new house will be finished)*

PAGE 8 How do you think the girl feels about talking on the phone? *(Possible response: She is smiling, so she probably likes it.)*

TEXT-TO-WORLD QUESTION
What would you do if you lived somewhere in the world that does not have telephones?

REVISIT THE BOOK
THINK AND SHARE
Answers
1. Possible responses: Telephones help people talk to other people at work. They help people talk about what work needs to be done.
2. Possible responses: Telephones help us talk to family and friends at home. We can use them to get information.
3. Possible responses: It would be very hard. We would need to write letters or drive to see them.

EXTEND UNDERSTANDING Explain how people communicated before telephones were invented. Ask children to name other ways they communicate besides using the telephone.

RESPONSE OPTIONS

ART Have children fold a sheet of paper in half. On one half, have them draw themselves on the phone. On the other half, have them draw the person they're talking to. Then have children label each person on their drawing.

SOCIAL STUDIES CONNECTION

Plan a walk through the school. Plan ahead to talk to the adults in each area and have children ask them whom they talk to on the phone. Then go back to the classroom and record and discuss the responses.

GRAPHIC ORGANIZER, PAGE 78
Help children complete the web to show some of the people a telephone helps us keep in touch with. Children may draw pictures and/ or write words to complete the web. *(Possible responses: doctor, teacher, librarian, builder, vet, friends)*

Name_____

Fill in the web to show who you can talk to using a telephone.

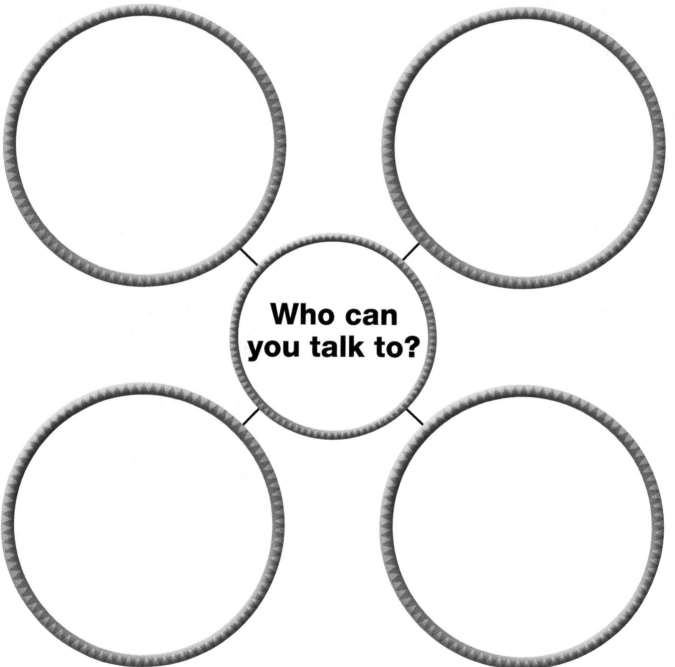

Who can you talk to?

Let's Plant a Garden

SUMMARY Children read about what people do to plant a garden.

VOCABULARY
High-Frequency Words

someone	have	a
some	the	our

Concept Words

idea	garden	brings
dirt	dig	seeds
gloves	weed	remember

INTRODUCE THE BOOK

BUILD BACKGROUND Discuss with children different types of gardens and how a garden is maintained.

ELL Write the concept words on the board. Read them aloud with the children. Display magnetic alphabet letters on a large magnetic board. Have children choose a concept word and use the magnetic letters to spell the word. Then have them read the word aloud.

PREVIEW Invite children to take a picture walk to preview the text and photos in the book. Discuss what is shown on each page.

READ THE BOOK

SET PURPOSE Have children set a purpose for reading *Let's Plant a Garden*. Ask them to think about why planting a garden is good idea for a neighborhood.

COMPREHENSION QUESTIONS

PAGE 5 Where is the girl planting the seeds? *(Possible responses: in the garden; in the dirt)*

PAGE 6 Why do you think the boy is watering the garden? *(Possible responses: because plants need water to grow)*

PAGE 8 Why does the girl want to remember the garden? *(Possible responses: because in the winter it will go away; it might not look the same next year)*

TEXT-TO-SELF QUESTION

What gardens have you seen? What did you notice about them?

REVISIT THE BOOK

THINK AND SHARE
Answers
1. an idea to plant a garden
2. Possible responses: They brought dirt and dug. They brought seeds and planted. They brought water and watered the garden. They brought gloves and weeded. They brought a camera and took a picture.
3. Possible responses: They could take care of the garden; they could clean up a park; they could fix up a house; they could plant flowers at a school.

EXTEND UNDERSTANDING Explain to children that the plants and vegetables in a garden are planted in sections. Then talk about what a garden needs to grow.

RESPONSE OPTIONS

WRITING Have children write a sentence about what they would do to help plant a garden. Then have them illustrate their sentences.

SCIENCE CONNECTION

Display a large felt board. Have a variety of plant, fruit, and vegetable shapes in felt form—3–4 shapes for each item. Have children plan a garden. Have them label each part of the garden with what is planted there.

GRAPHIC ORGANIZER, PAGE 80

Help children complete the chart to show the tool needed to do the job. Children can write the word or draw the picture that goes with each garden item. (Responses: dirt—shovel, seeds—trowel or hands, water—watering can or hose, weeds—garden gloves, photo—camera)

Name_____

Fill in the chart to tell what tools are needed.

What tool do we need?

T-Chart

Suggestions You can use this chart to record information in two categories or for various sorting activities. Write the heading at the top of each column.

Three-Column Chart

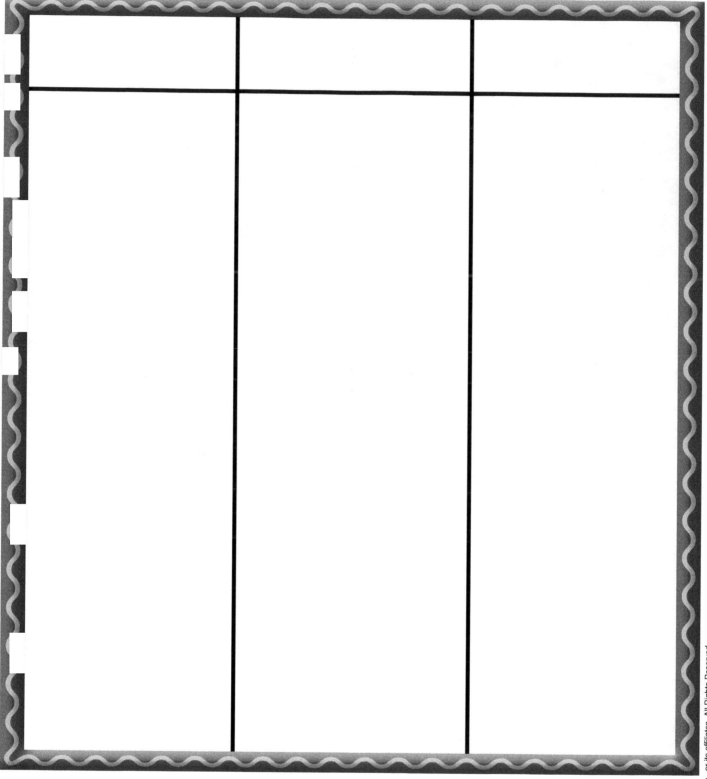

Suggestions You can use this chart to record information in three categories or for various sorting activities. Write the heading at the top of each column.

Classify

Suggestions Children can use this chart to classify information. For example, pictures of animals could be placed in the circle and then sorted into land animals and water animals in the boxes below.

Pictograph

Title _____

Suggestions Help children make a pictograph to record information. Children draw simple pictures on the chart or on self-stick notes to represent each item. Record the topic at the top of the chart. Some possible topics are: *What did we have for lunch? What pets do we have? What color shoes are we wearing?*

Web A

Suggestions You can use this chart to activate children's prior knowledge about a topic. Write a major concept in the circle such as *Pets* or *Machines.* Children write or dictate words or ideas that relate to the concept. Write them so that the lines connect them to the circle.

Web B

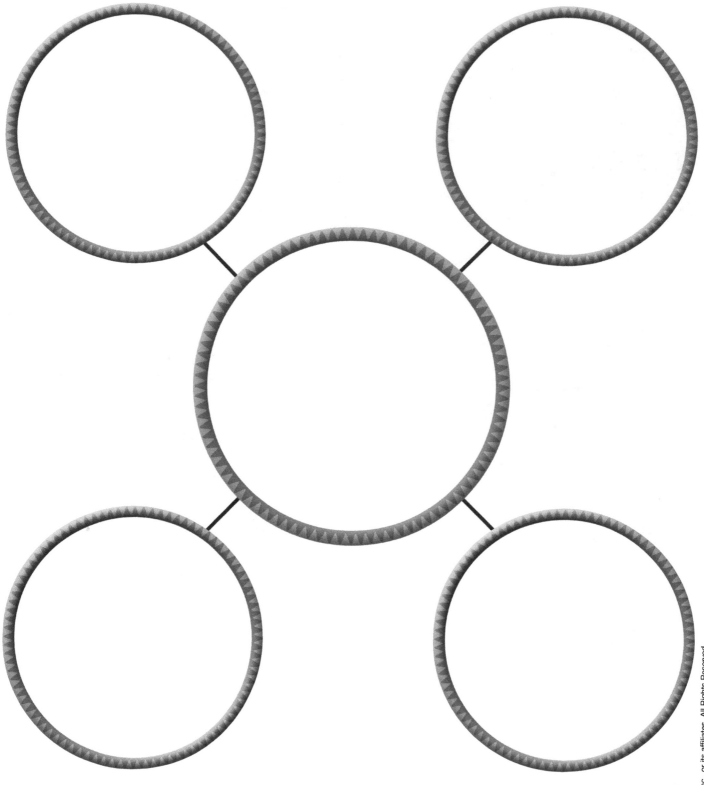

Suggestions You can use this chart to activate children's prior knowledge about a topic. Write a major concept in the middle circle, such as *Things at School*. In the smaller circles, children dictate words or ideas that relate to the concept. Additional ideas may be added on spokes coming from the smaller circles.

KWL Chart

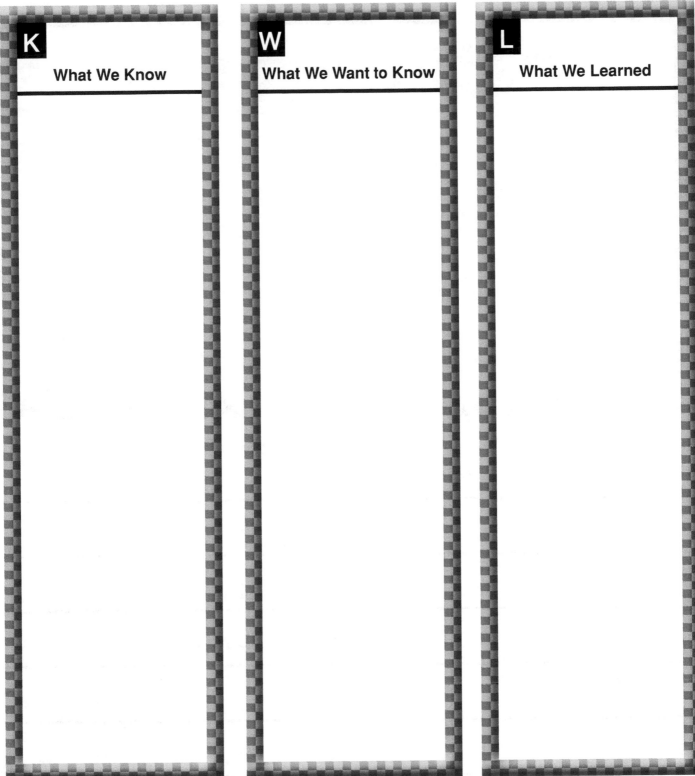

K	W	L
What We Know	**What We Want to Know**	**What We Learned**

Suggestions Have children tell what they know or think they know about the topic. Record their responses in the column **What We Know.** Ask children what they would like to learn. List their questions in **What We Want to Know.** After children learn more about the topic, discuss what they learned. List children's responses in **What We Learned.**

Prediction

Suggestions You can use this chart to help children discuss predictions. Have children suggest what might happen next in a story or other situation. Children may draw a picture and dictate sentences to show the prediction.

Sequence

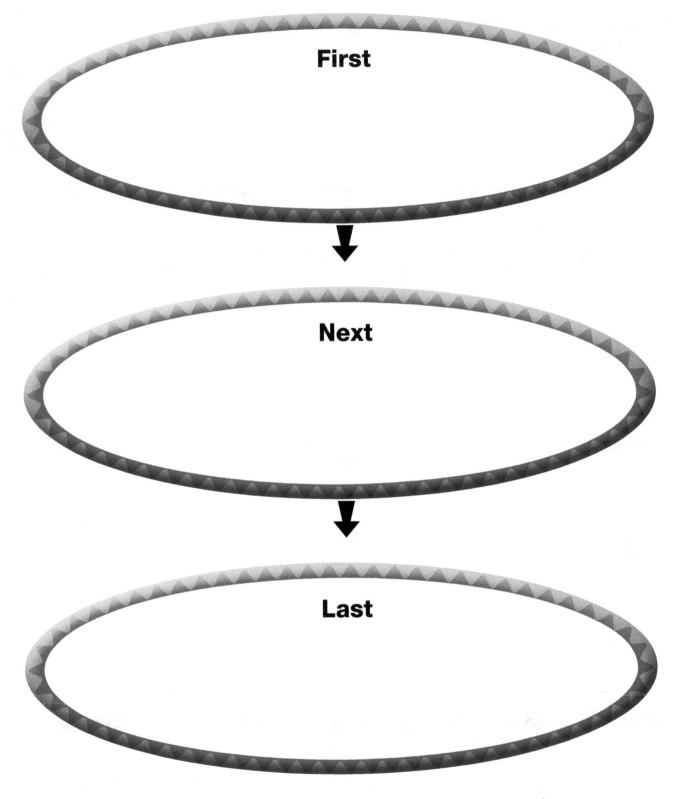

First

Next

Last

Suggestions Use this chart to help children place events in sequence. Children can draw pictures or dictate what happened first, next, and last.

Story Sequence A

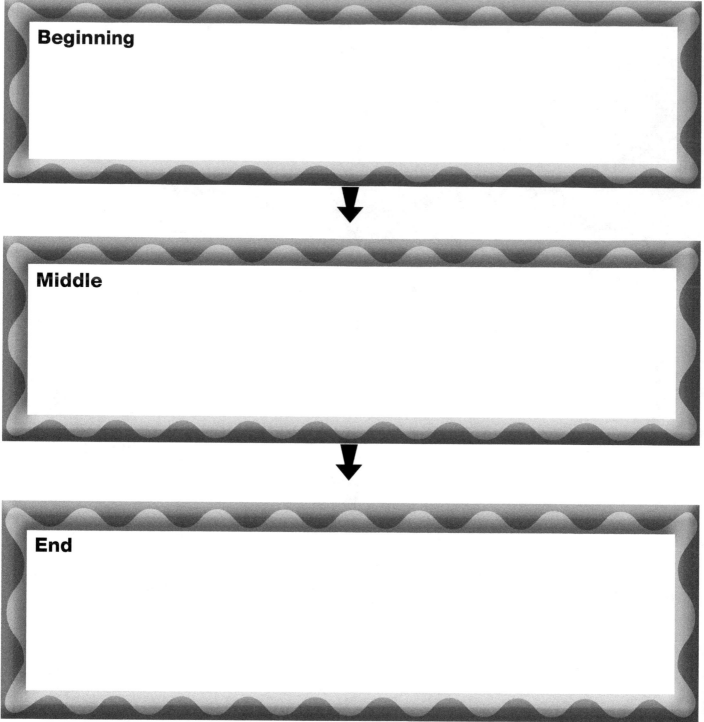

Beginning

Middle

End

Suggestions Use this chart to help children place events in a story in sequence. Children can draw pictures or dictate what happened in the beginning, middle, and end.

Story Sequence B

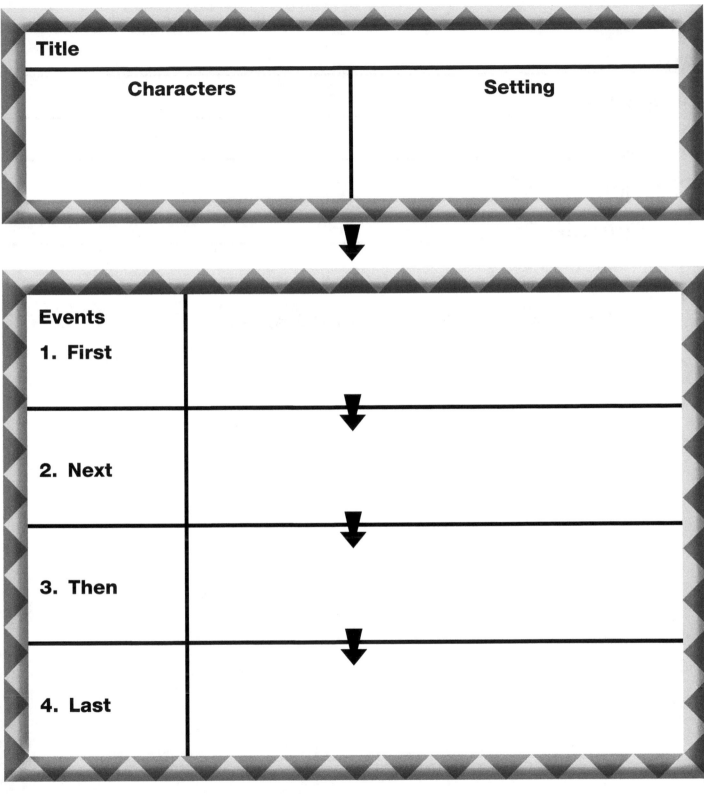

Title	
Characters	**Setting**

Events	
1. First	
2. Next	
3. Then	
4. Last	

Suggestions After recording the title, characters, and setting of a story, children chart the sequence of events. This organizer helps children understand how one event leads to another.

Book Report

Title _____

Author _____

Illustrator _____

Setting _____

Characters _____

Our Favorite Parts _____

Suggestions You can use this chart to record information about a big book or trade book. Discuss where the story takes place, what happens in the book, and how children feel about the book. Invite children to draw pictures of their favorite parts of the book.

Story Comparison

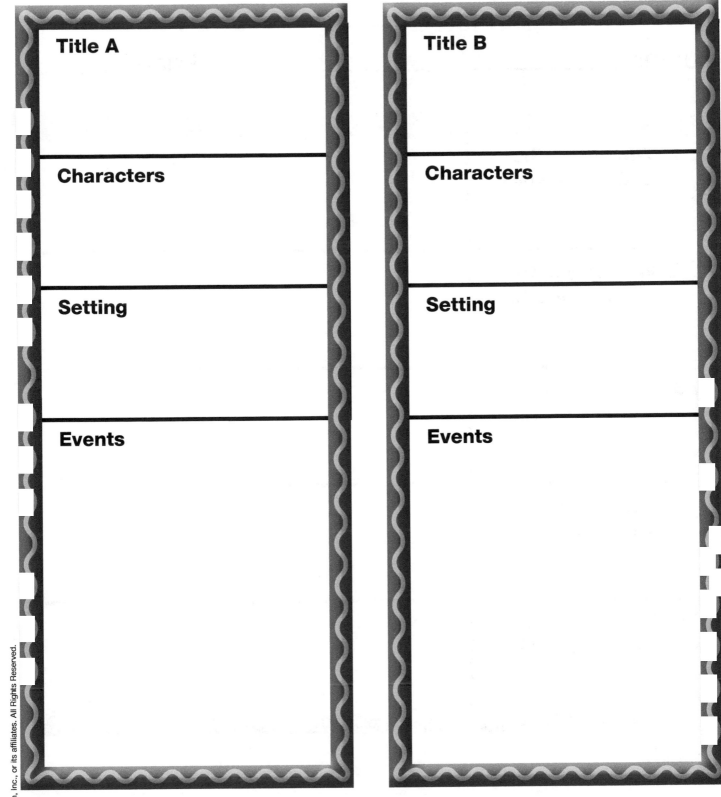

Title A

Characters

Setting

Events

Title B

Characters

Setting

Events

Suggestions Use this chart to help children compare story elements and structures. This type of activity prepares children for working with Venn diagrams. Children may illustrate or dictate these comparisons.

Question the Author

Title _____

Author _____ Page _____

1. What does the author tell you?	
2. Why do you think the author tells you that?	
3. Does the author say it clearly?	
4. What would make it clearer?	
5. How would you say it instead?	

Suggestions Use this chart to help children understand the author's purpose and the author's craft. Students analyze what was said, how well it was said, and how it might be said differently.

Main Idea

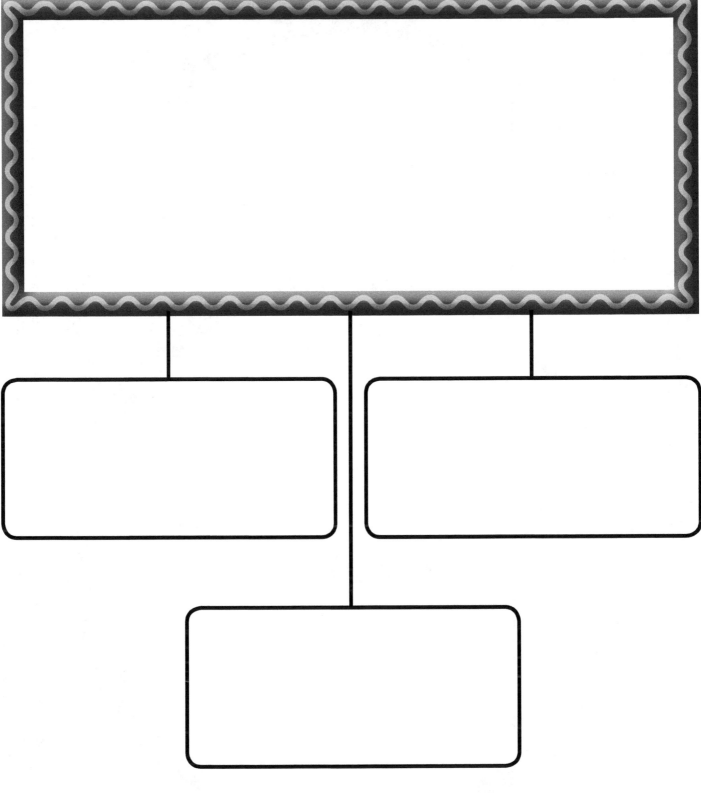

Suggestions Use this chart to help children understand the main idea of what they read. Ask: *What is the story all about?* Write children's responses in the top box. Have children draw or dictate in the smaller boxes other things they remember from the story.

Venn Diagram

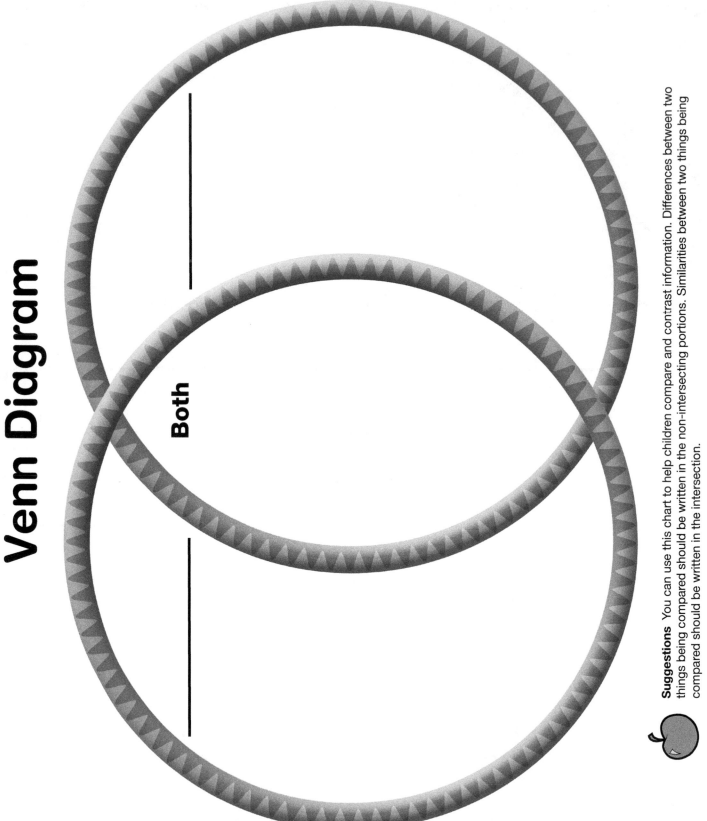

Both

Cause and Effect

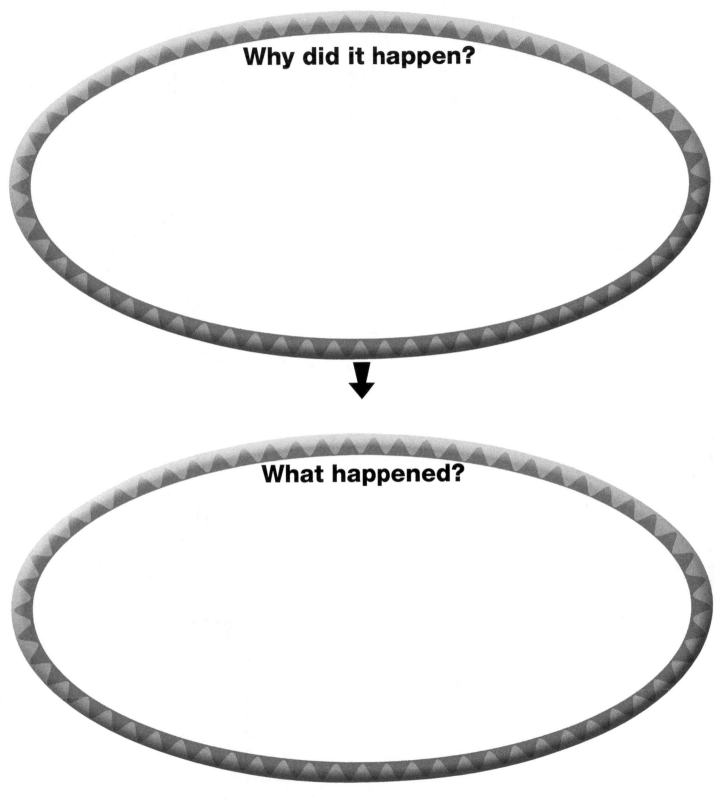

Why did it happen?

What happened?

Suggestions Use this chart to help children understand what happens (effect) and why it happens (cause). Children draw pictures in the appropriate ovals or dictate sentences to show an event. Help children think back and describe or draw what caused that event to happen.

Cycle Chart

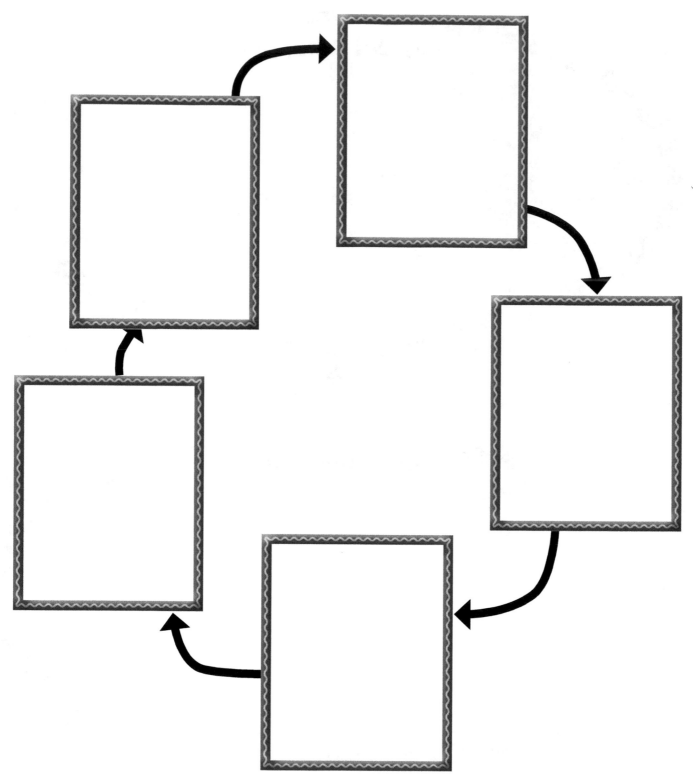

![apple] **Suggestions** Use this chart to help children understand how a series of events produces a series of results again and again. Discuss such questions as: *How does one event lead to another? What is the final outcome?* This chart works well for depicting life cycles.

Steps in a Process

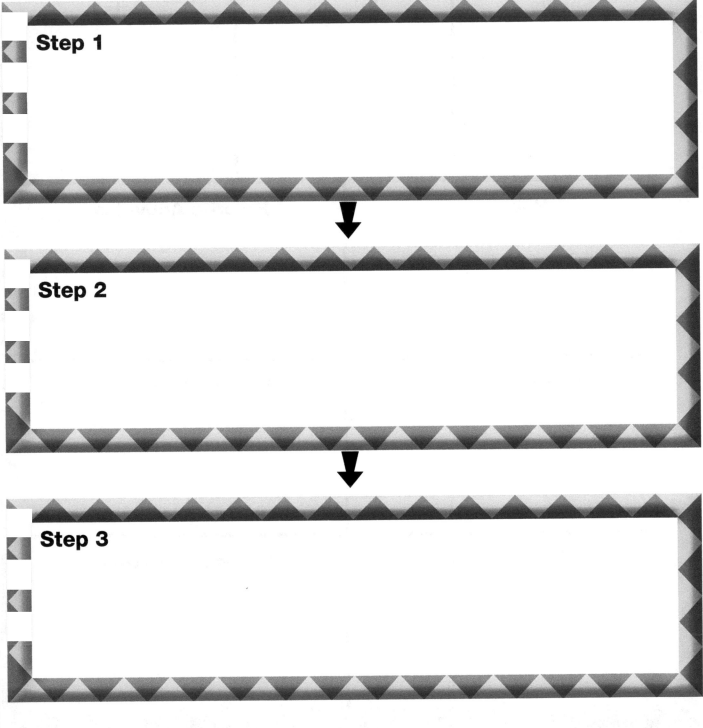

Step 1

Step 2

Step 3

Suggestions Use this chart to help children break down a process. This chart works well with a how-to activity that has a few simple steps. Students may draw pictures or dictate how to do something.

Writing Topics

Family	Friends	Pets

Hobbies	Favorite Activities

Special Places	Favorite Vacations

Happy Times	Times I Felt Proud

Suggestions Use this chart as a writing resource or interest inventory. Over time, children can generate numerous topics for future compositions.

Letter Format

Dear _____ ,

_____

_____

_____

_____

_____

_____

_____

_____

_____

_____ ,

_____

Suggestions Use this organizer to help children understand the format of a letter. The format can be used for writing to friends, family, or characters from a story.

Numbered List

Title _____

1. _____

2. _____

3. _____

4. _____

5. _____